THE CHARLES G. FINNEY
MEMORIAL LIBRARY

Evangelistic Sermon Series
- So Great Salvation
- The Guilt of Sin
- True and False Repentance
- God's Love for a Sinning World

Revival Sermon Series
- Victory Over the World
- True Saints
- True Submission

**GOD'S LOVE
for a SINNING WORLD**

GOD'S LOVE for a SINNING WORLD

Evangelistic Messages

CHARLES G. FINNEY

KREGEL PUBLICATIONS
GRAND RAPIDS, MICHIGAN 49503

Library of Congress Catalog Card Number 66-19200

This series of sermons selected from
SERMONS ON GOSPEL THEMES
by Charles G. Finney

Printed in the United States of America

PUBLISHER'S FOREWORD

Why this new edition of the sermons of Charles Grandison Finney? Because in many ways the days in which we are living are a duplicate of the day and situation in which Finney himself proclaimed the message which God had given him — the call to evangelism and to revival. These messages speak to our day in no uncertain sound for conditions within the church, and in the world around, call for a voice from God, a resounding clarion call for return to the Biblical standard of Christian life, and the God-ordained plan of redemption and revival.

These have been chosen and arranged with the needs of the world and church today in view. They are as applicable in this day of falling away and departure from the faith as they were in Finney's day. Heart-searching and uncompromising, they cut away the froth and frills so apparent in much modern preaching to reveal God's message for a sinning world, a world seemingly intent upon self-destruction and self-aggrandizement.

It is the publisher's prayer that these messages in their new form will convey God's message to our needy world, revealing His will and purpose for His Church — and His divine plan of salvation for an unbelieving generation.

The Publishers

CONTENTS

1

GOD'S LOVE
FOR A SINNING WORLD

"For God so loved the world that he gave his only begotten Son, that whosoever believeth in Him should not perish, but have everlasting life."—John 3 : 16

SIN is the most expensive thing in the universe. Nothing else can cost so much. Pardoned or unpardoned, its cost is infinitely great. Pardoned, the cost falls chiefly on the great atoning Substitute; unpardoned, it must fall on the head of the guilty sinner.

The existence of sin is a fact everywhere experienced—everywhere observed. There *is* sin in our race everywhere and in awful aggravation.

Sin is the violation of an infinitely important law—a law designed and adapted to secure the highest good of the universe. Obedience to this law is naturally essential to the good of creatures. Without obedience there could be no blessedness even in heaven.

As sin is a violation of a most important law, it cannot be treated lightly. No government can afford to treat disobedience as a trifle, inasmuch as everything—the entire welfare of the government and of all the governed—turns upon obedience. Just in proportion to the value of the interests at stake is the necessity of guarding law and of punishing disobedience.

The law of God must not be dishonoured by anything *He* shall do. It has been dishonoured by the disobedience of man ; hence, the more need that God should stand by it, to retrieve its honour.   The utmost dishonour is done to law by disowning, disobeying, and despising it,   All this, sinning man has done.   Hence, this law being not only good, but intrinsically necessary to the happiness of the governed, it becomes of all things most necessary that the law-giver should vindicate his law.   He must by all means do it.

Hence, sin has involved God's government in a vast expense. Either the law must be executed at the expense of the well-being of the whole race, or God must submit to suffer the worst results of disrespect to His law—results which in some form must involve a vast expense.

Take for example any human government.   Suppose the righteous and necessary laws which it imposes are disowned and dishonoured.   In such a case the violated law must be honoured by the execution of its penalty, or something else not less expensive, and probably much more so, must be endured.   Transgression must cost happiness, somewhere, and in vast amount.

In the case of God's government it has been deemed advisable to provide a substitute—one that should answer the purpose of saving the sinner, and yet of honouring the law. This being determined on, the next great question was—*How shall the expense be met ?*

The Bible informs us how the question was in fact decided.   By a voluntary conscription—shall I call it—or donation ?   Call it as we may, it was a voluntary offering. Who shall head the subscription ?   Who shall begin where so much is to be raised ?   Who will make the first sacrifice ? Who will take the first step in a project so vast ?   The Bible informs us.   It began with the Infinite Father.   He made the first great donation.   He gave His only begotten Son—this to begin with—and having given Him first, He freely gives all else that the exigencies of the case can require.   First, He gave His Son to make the atonement due to law ; then gave and sent His Holy Spirit to take charge of this work. The Son on His part consented to stand as the representative of sinners, that He might honour the law, by suffering in their stead. He poured out His blood, made a whole life of suffering a free donation on the altar—withheld not His face from spitting, nor His back from stripes—shrunk not from the utmost contumely that wicked men could heap on Him. So the Holy Ghost also devotes Himself to most self-denying efforts unceasingly, to accomplish the great object.

It would have been a very short method to have turned over His hand upon the wicked of our race, and sent them all down quick to hell, as once He did when certain angels "kept not their first estate." Rebellion broke out in heaven. Not long did God bear it, around His lofty throne. But in the case of man He changed His course—did not send them all to hell, but devised a vast scheme of measures, involving most amazing self-denials and self-sacrifices, to gain men's souls back to obedience and heaven.

For whom was this great donation made? "God so loved the *World*," meaning the whole race of men. By the "world" in this connection cannot be meant any particular part only, but the whole race. Not only the Bible, but the nature of the case, shows that the atonement must have been made for the whole world. For plainly if it had not been made for the entire race, no man of the race could ever know that it was made for himself, and therefore not a man could believe on Christ in the sense of receiving by faith the blessings of the atonement. There being an utter uncertainty as to the persons embraced in the limited provisions which we now *suppose* to be made, the entire donation must fail through the impossibility of rational faith for its reception. Suppose a will is made by a rich man bequeathing certain property to certain unknown persons, described only by the name of "the elect." They are not described otherwise than by this term, and all agree that although the maker of the will had the individuals definitely in his mind, yet that he left no description of them, which either the persons themselves, the courts, nor any living mortal can understand. Now such a will is of necessity altogether null and void. No living man can claim under such a will, and none the better though these elect were described as residents of Oberlin. Since it does not embrace all the residents of Oberlin, and does not define which of them, all is lost. All having an equal claim and none any definite claim, none can inherit. If the atonement were made in this way, no living man would have any valid reason for believing himself one of the elect, prior to his reception of the Gospel. Hence he would have no authority to believe and receive its blessings by faith. In fact, the atonement must be wholly void—on this supposition—unless a special revelation is made to the persons for whom it is intended.

As the case is, however, the very fact that a man belongs to the race of Adam—the fact that he is human, born of woman, is all-sufficient. It brings him within the pale. He is one of the *world* for whom God gave His Son, that whosoever would believe in Him might not perish, but have everlasting life.

The subjective motive in the mind of God for this great gift was *love*, love to the world. God so loved the world that He gave His Son to die for it. God loved the universe also, but this gift of His Son sprang from love to our world. True in this great act He took pains to provide for the interests of the universe. He was careful to do nothing that could in the least let down the sacredness of His law. Most carefully did He intend to guard against misapprehension as to His regard for His law and for the high interests of obedience and happiness in his moral universe. He meant once for all to preclude the danger lest any moral agent should be tempted to undervalue the moral law.

Yet farther, it was not only from love to souls, but from respect to the spirit of the law of His own eternal reason, that He gave up His Son to die. In this the purpose to give up His Son originated. The law of His own reason must be honoured and held sacred. He may do nothing inconsistent with its spirit. He must do everything possible to prevent the commission of sin and to secure the confidence and love of His subjects. So sacred did He hold these great objects that He would baptize His Son in His own blood, sooner than peril the good of the universe. Beyond a question it was love and regard for the highest good of the universe that led Him to sacrifice His own beloved Son.

Let us next consider attentively the *nature* of this love. The text lays special stress on this—God *so* loved—His love was of such a nature, so wonderful and so peculiar in its character, that it led Him to give up His only Son to die. More is evidently implied in this expression than simply its greatness. It is most peculiar in its character. Unless we understand this, we shall be in danger of falling into the strange mistake of the Universalists, who are forever talking about God's love for sinners, but whose notions of the nature of this love never lead to repentance or to holiness. They seem to think of this love as simply good nature, and conceive of God only as a very good-natured being, whom nobody need to fear. Such notions have not the least influence towards holiness, but the very opposite. It is only when we come to understand what this love is in its nature that we feel its moral power promoting holiness.

It may be reasonably asked, If God so loved the world with a love characterized by greatness, and by greatness only, why did He not save all the world without sacrificing His Son? This question suffices to show us that there is deep meaning in this word *so*, and should put us upon a careful study of this meaning.

1. This love in its nature is not *complacency*—a delight in the character of the race. This could not be, for there was nothing amiable in their character. For God to have loved such a race *complacently* would have been infinitely disgraceful to Himself.

2. It was not a mere emotion or feeling. It was not a blind impulse, though many seem to suppose it was. It seems to be often supposed that God acted as men do when they are borne away by strong emotion. But there could be no virtue in this. A man might give away all he is worth under such a blind impulse of feeling, and be none the more virtuous. But in saying this we do not exclude all emotion from the love of benevolence, nor from God's love for a lost world. He had emotion, but not emotion *only*. Indeed, the Bible everywhere teaches us that God's love for man, lost in his sins, was paternal—the love of a father for his offspring—in this case, for a rebellious, froward, prodigal offspring. In this love there must of course blend the deepest compassion.

3. On the part of Christ, considered as Mediator, this love was *fraternal*. " He is not ashamed to call them *brethren*." In one point of view, He is acting for brethren, and in another for children. The Father gave Him up for this work and of course sympathizes in the love appropriate to its relations.

4. This love must be altogether *disinterested*, for He had nothing to hope or to fear—no profit to make out of His children if they should be saved. Indeed, it is impossible to conceive of God as being selfish, since His love embraces all creatures and all interests according to their real value. No doubt He took delight in saving our race—why should He not ? It is a great salvation in every sense, and greatly does it swell the bliss of heaven—greatly will it affect the glory and the blessedness of the Infinite God. He will eternally respect Himself for love so disinterested. He knows also

that all His Holy creatures will eternally respect Him for this work and for the love that gave it birth. But let it also be said, He knew they would not respect Him for this great work unless they should see that He did it for the good of sinners.

5. This love was *zealous*—not that cold-hearted state of mind which some suppose—not an abstraction, but a love deep, zealous, earnest, burning in his soul as a fire that nothing can quench.

6. The sacrifice was a most self-denying one. Did it cost the Father nothing to give up His own beloved Son to suffer, and to die such a death? If this be not self-denial, what can be? Thus to give up His Son to so much suffering—is not this the noblest self-denial? The universe never could have the idea of great self-denial but for such an exemplification.

7. This love was particular because it was universal; and also universal because it was particular. God loved each sinner in particular, and therefore loved all. Because He loved all impartially, with no respect of persons, therefore He loved each in particular.

8. This was a most *patient* love. How rare to find a parent so loving his child as never to be impatient. Let me go round and ask, how many of you, parents, can say that you love all your children so well, and with so much love, and with love so wisely controlling, that you have never felt impatient towards any of them—so that you can take them in your arms under the greatest provocations and love them *down*, love them out of their sins, love them into repentance and into a filial spirit? Of which of your children can you say, Thank God, I never fretted against that child—of which, if you were to meet him in heaven, could you say, I never caused that child to fret? Often have I heard parents say, I love my children, but oh, how my patience fails me! And, after the dear ones are dead, you may hear their bitter

moans, Oh, my soul, how could I have caused my child so much stumbling and so much sin !

But God never frets—is never impatient. His love is so deep and so great that He is always patient.

Sometimes, when parents have unfortunate children—poor objects of compassion—they can bear with anything from them ; but when they are very wicked, they seem to feel that they are quite excusable for being impatient. In God's case, these are not unfortunate children, but are intensely wicked —intelligently wicked. But oh, His amazing patience—so set upon their good, so desirous of their highest welfare, that however they abuse Him, He sets Himself to bless them still, and weep them down, and melt them into penitence and love, by the death of His Son in their stead !

9. This is a *jealous love*, not in a bad sense, but in a good sense—in the sense of being exceedingly careful lest anything should occur to injure those He loves. Just as husband and wife who truly love each other are jealous with ever wakeful jealousy over each other's welfare, seeking always to do all they can to promote each other's true interests.

This donation is already made—made in good faith—not only *promised*, but actually *made*. The promise, given long before, has been fulfilled. The Son has come, has died, has made the ransom and lives to offer it—a prepared salvation to all who will embrace it.

The Son of God died not to appease vengeance, as some seem to understand it, but under the demands of law. The law had been dishonoured by its violation. Hence, Christ undertook to honour it by giving up to its demands His suffering life and atoning death. It was not to appease a vindictive spirit in God, but to secure the highest good of the universe in a dispensation of mercy.

Since this atonement has been made, all men in the race have a right to it. It is open to every one who will embrace it. Though Jesus still remains the Father's Son, yet by

gracious right He belongs in an important sense to the race—
to everyone ; so that every sinner has an interest in His
blood if he will only come humbly forward and claim it.
God sent His Son to be the Saviour of the world—of whomsoever would believe and accept this great salvation.

God gives His Spirit to apply this salvation to men. He
comes to each man's door and knocks, to gain admittance, if
He can, and show each sinner that he may now have salvation. Oh, what a labour of love is this !

This salvation must be received, if at all, *by faith*. This
is the only possible way. God's government over sinners is
moral, not physical, because the sinner is himself a moral
and not a physical agent. Therefore, God can influence us
in no way unless we will give Him our confidence. He never
can save us by merely taking us away to some place called
heaven—as if change of place would change the voluntary
heart. There can, therefore, be no possible way to be saved
but by simple faith.

Now do not mistake and suppose that embracing the
Gospel is simply to believe these historical facts without truly
receiving Christ as *your* Saviour. If this had been the
scheme, then Christ had need only to come down and die ;
then go back to heaven and quietly wait to see who would
believe the facts. But how different is the real case ! Now
Christ comes down to fill the soul with His own life and love.
Penitent sinners hear and believe the truth concerning Jesus,
and then receive Christ into the soul to live and reign there
supreme and for ever. On this point many mistake, saying,
If I believe the facts as matters of history it is enough.
No ! no ! This is not it by any means. " *With the heart*
man believeth unto righteousness." The atonement was
indeed made to provide the way so that Jesus could come
down to human hearts and draw them into union and sympathy with Himself—so that God could let down the arms
of His love and embrace sinners—so that law and govern-

ment should not be dishonoured by such tokens of friendship shown by God toward sinners. But the atonement will by no means save sinners only as it prepares the way for them to come into sympathy and fellowship of heart with God.

Now Jesus comes to each sinner's door and knocks. Hark! what's that? what's that? Why this knocking? Why did He not go away and stay in heaven if that were the system, till men should simply believe the historical facts and be baptized, as some suppose, for salvation. But now, see how He comes down—tells the sinner what He has done—reveals all His love—tells him how holy and sacred it is, so sacred that He can by no means act without reference to the holiness of His law and the purity of His government. Thus impressing on the heart the most deep and enlarged ideas of His holiness and purity, He enforces the need of deep repentance and the sacred duty of renouncing all sin.

CONCLUSION

1. The Bible teaches that sinners may forfeit their birthright and put themselves beyond the reach of mercy. It is not long since I made some remark to you on the manifest necessity that God should guard Himself against the abuses of His love. The circumstances are such as create the greatest danger of such abuse, and, therefore, He must make sinners know that they may not abuse His love, and cannot do it with inpunity.

2. Under the Gospel, sinners are in circumstances of the greatest possible responsibility. They are in the utmost danger of trampling down beneath their feet the very Son of God. Come, they say, let us kill Him and the inheritance shall be ours. When God sends forth, last of all, His own beloved Son, what do they do? Add to all their other sins and rebellions the highest insult to this glorious Son! Suppose something analogous to this were done under a human government. A case of rebellion occurs in some of the

provinces. The king sends his own son, not with an army, to cut them down quick in their rebellion, but all gently, meekly, patiently, he goes among them, explaining the laws of the kingdom and exhorting them to obedience.   What do they do in the case? With one consent they combine to seize him and put him to death !

But you deny the application of this, and ask me, Who murdered the Son of God? Were they not Jews? Aye, and have you, sinners, had no part in this murder? Has not your treatment of Jesus Christ shown that you are most fully in sympathy with the ancient Jews in their murder of the Son of God? If you had been there, would any one have shouted louder than you, Away with Him—crucify Him, crucify Him ? Have you not always said, Depart from us—for we desire not the knowledge of Thy ways ?

3. It was said of Christ that, Though rich He became poor that we through His poverty might be rich. How strikingly true is this? Our redemption cost Christ His life ; it found Him rich, but made Him poor ; it found us infinitely poor, but made us rich even to all the wealth of heaven. But of these riches none can partake till they shall each for himself accept them in the legitimate way. They must be received on the terms proposed, or the offer passes utterly away, and you are left poorer even than if no such treasures had ever been laid at your feet.

Many persons seem entirely to misconceive this case. They seem not to believe what God says, but keep saying, *If, if, if* there only were any salvation for me—*if* there were only an atonement provided for the pardon of my sins. This was one of the last things that was cleared up in my mind before I fully committed my soul to trust God. I had been studying the atonement ; I saw its philosophical bearings— saw what it demanded of the sinner ; but it irritated me, and I said—If I should become a Christian, how could I know what God would do with me ? Under this irritation

I said foolish and bitter things against Christ—till my own soul was horrified at its own wickedness, and I said—I will make all this up with Christ if the thing is possible.

In this way many advance upon the encouragements of the Gospel as if it were only a peradventure, an *experiment*. They take each forward step most carefully, with fear and trembling, as if there were the utmost doubt whether there could be any mercy for them. So with myself. I was on my way to my office, when the question came before my mind—What are you waiting for? You need not get up such an ado. All is done already. You have only to consent to the proposition—give your heart right up to it at once—this is all. Just so it is. All Christians and sinners ought to understand that the whole plan is complete—that the whole of Christ—His character, His work, His atoning death, and His ever-living intercession—belong to each and every man, and need only to be accepted. There is a full ocean of it. *There* it is. You may just as well take it as not. It is as if you stood on the shore of an ocean of soft, pure water, famishing with thirst; you are welcome to drink, and you need not fear lest you exhaust that ocean, or starve anybody else by drinking yourself. You need not feel that you are not made free to that ocean of waters; you are invited and pressed to drink—yea, to *drink abundantly!* This ocean supplies all your need. You do not need to have in yourself the attributes of Jesus Christ, for His attributes become practically yours for all possible use. As saith the Scripture—He is of God made unto us wisdom, righteousness, sanctification, and redemption. What do you need? Wisdom? Here it is. Righteousness? Here it is. Sanctification? Here you have it. All is in Christ. Can you possibly think of any one thing needful for your moral purity, or your usefulness which is not here in Christ? Nothing. All is provided here. Therefore you need not say, I will go and pray and try, as the hymn,—

> " I'll go to Jesus tho' my sin
> Hath like a mountain rose,
> *Perhaps* He will admit my plea ;
> *Perhaps* will hear my prayer."

There is no need of any *perhaps*. The doors are always open. Like the doors of Broadway Tabernacle in New York, made to swing open and fasten themselves open, so that they could not swing back and shut down upon the crowds of people thronging to pass through. When they were to be made, I went myself to the workmen and told them by all means to fix them so that they must swing open and fasten themselves in that position.

So the door of salvation is open always—fastened open, and no man can shut it—not the Pope, even, nor the devil, nor any angel from heaven or from hell. There it stands, all swung back and the passage wide open for every sinner of our race to enter if he will.

Again, sin is the most expensive thing in the universe. Are you well aware, O sinner, what a price has been paid for you that you may be redeemed and made an heir of God and of heaven ? O what an expensive business for you to indulge in sin !

And what an enormous tax the government of God has paid to redeem this province from its ruin ! Talk about the poor tax of Great Britain and of all other nations superadded ; all is nothing to the sin-tax of Jehovah's government—that awful *sin-tax !* Think how much machinery is kept in motion to save sinners ! The Son of God was sent down—angels are sent as ministering spirits to the heirs of salvation ; missionaries are sent, Christians labour, and pray and weep in deep and anxious solicitude—all to seek and save the lost. What a wonderful—enormous tax is levied upon the benevolence of the universe to put away sin and to save the sinner ! If the cost could be computed in solid gold what a world of it—a solid globe of itself ! What an array of toil and cost, from angels, Jesus Christ, the Divine Spirit, and living men ! Shame on sinners who hold on to sin despite of all these benevolent efforts to save them ! who instead of being ashamed out of sin, will say—Let God pay off this tax ; who cares ! Let the missionaries labour, let pious women work their very fingers off to raise funds to keep all this human machinery in motion ; no matter : what is all this to me ? I have loved my pleasures and after them I will go ! What an unfeeling heart is this !

Sinners can very well afford to make sacrifices to save their fellow sinners. Paul could for his fellow sinners. He felt that he had done his part toward making sinners, and now it became him to do his part also in converting them back to God. But see there—that young man thinks he cannot afford to be a minister, for he is afraid he shall not be well supported. Does he not owe something to the grace that saved his soul from hell ?. Has he not some sacrifices to make, since Jesus has made so many for him, and Christians too, in Christ before him—did they not pray and suffer and toil for his soul's salvation ? As to his danger of lacking bread in the Lord's work, let him trust his Great Master. Yet let me also say that churches may be in great fault for not comfortably supporting their pastors. Let them know God will assuredly starve them if they starve their ministers. Their own souls and the souls of their children shall be barren as death if they avariciously starve those whom God in His providence sends to feed them with the bread of life.

How much it costs to rid society of certain forms of sin, as for example, *slavery.* How much has been expended already, and how much more yet remains to be expended ere this sore evil and curse and sin shall be rooted from our land ! This is part of God's great enterprise, and He will press it on to its completion. Yet at what an amazing cost ! How many lives and how much agony to get rid of this one sin !

Woe to those who make capital out of the sins of men! Just think of the rumseller—tempting men while God is trying to dissuade them from rushing on in the ways of sin and death! Think of the guilt of those who thus set themselves in array against God! So Christ has to contend with rumsellers who are doing all they can to hinder His work.

Our subject strikingly illustrates the nature of sin as mere selfishness. It cares not how much sin costs Jesus Christ —how much it costs the Church, how much it taxes the benevolent sympathies and the self-sacrificing labours of all the good in earth or heaven;—no matter; the sinner loves self-indulgence and will have it while he can. How many of you have cost your friends countless tears and trouble to get you back from your ways of sin? Are you not ashamed when so much has been done for you, that you cannot be persuaded to give up your sins and turn to God and holiness?

The whole effort on the part of God for man is one of suffering and self-denial. Beginning with the sacrifice of His own beloved Son, it is carried on with ever renewed sacrifices and toilsome labours—at great and wonderful expense. Just think how long a *time* these efforts have been protracted already—how many tears, poured out like water, it has cost—how much *pain* in many forms this enterprise has caused and cost—yea, that very sin which you roll as a sweet morsel under your tongue! God may well hate it when He sees how much it costs, and say—O do not that abominable thing that I hate!

Yet God is not unhappy in these self-denials. So great is His joy in the results, that He deems all the suffering but comparatively a trifle, even as earthly parents enjoy the efforts they make to bless their children. See them; they will almost work their very hands off;—mothers sit up at night to ply their needle till they reel with fatigue and blindness; but if you were to see their toil, you would often see also their joy, so intensely do they love their children.

Such is the labour, the joy, and the self-denial of the Father, the Son and the Holy Ghost, in their great work for human salvation. Often are they grieved that so many will refuse to be saved. Toiling on in a common sympathy, there is nothing, within reasonable limits, which they will not do or suffer to accomplish their great work. It is wonderful to think how all creation sympathizes, too, in this work and its necessary sufferings. Go back to the scene of Christ's sufferings. Could the sun in the heavens look down unmoved on such a scene? O no, he could not even behold it—but veiled his face from the sight! All nature seemed to put on her robes of deepest mourning. The scene was too much for even inanimate nature to bear. The sun turned his back and could not look down on such a spectacle!

The subject illustrates forcibly the worth of the soul. Think you God would have done all this if He had had those low views on this subject which sinners usually have?

Martyrs and saints enjoy their sufferings—filling up in themselves what is lacking of the sufferings of Christ; not in the atonement proper, but in the subordinate parts of the work to be done. It is the nature of true religion to love self-denial.

The results will fully justify all the expense. God had well counted the cost before He began. Long time before He formed a moral universe He knew perfectly what it must cost Him to redeem sinners, and He knew that the result would amply justify all the cost. He knew that a wonder of mercy would be wrought—that the suffering demanded of Christ, great as it was, would be endured; and that results infinitely glorious would accrue therefrom. He looked down the track of time into the distant ages—where, as the cycles rolled along, there might be seen the joys of redeemed saints, who are singing their songs and striking their harps anew with the everlasting song, through the long, *long*, LONG

eternity of their blessedness ;—and was not this enough for
the heart of infinite love to enjoy ?   And what do you think
of it, Christian ?   Will you say now, I am ashamed to ask to
be forgiven ?   How can I bear to receive such mercy !   It is
the price of blood, and how can I accept it ?   How can I make
Jesus so much expense ?

You are right in saying that you have cost Him great
expense—but the expense has been cheerfully met—the pain
has all been endured, and will not need to be endured again,
and it will cost none the more if you accept than if you
decline ; and moreover still, let it be considered Jesus Christ
has not acted unwisely ; He did not pay too much for the
soul's redemption — not a pang more than the interests of
God's government demanded and the worth of the soul would
justify.

O, when you come to see Him face to face, and tell Him
what you think of it—when you are some thousands of years
older than you are now, will you not adore that wisdom that
manages this scheme, and the infinite love in which it had
its birth ?   O what will you then say of that amazing conde-
scension that brought down Jesus to your rescue !   Say,
Christian, have you not often poured out your soul before
your Saviour in acknowledgment of what you have cost
Him, and there seemed to be a kind of lifting up as if the
very bottom of your soul were to rise, and you would pour
out your whole heart.   If anybody had seen you they would
have wondered what had happened to you that had so melted
your soul in gratitude and love.

Say now, sinner, will you sell your birthright ?   How much
will you take for it ?   How much will you take for your
interest in Christ ?   For how much will you sell your soul ?
Sell your Christ !   Of old they sold Him for thirty pieces of
silver ; and ever since, the heavens have been raining tears of
blood on our guilty world.   If you were to be asked by the
devil to fix the sum for which you would sell your soul, what

would be the price named? Lorenzo Dow once met a man as he was riding along a solitary road to fulfil an appointment, and said to him—Friend, have you ever prayed? No. How much will you take never to pray hereafter? One dollar. Dow paid it over, and rode on. The man put the money in his pocket, and passed on, *thinking*. The more he thought, the worse he felt. There, said he, I have sold my soul for one dollar! It must be that I have met the *devil!* Nobody else would tempt me so. With all my soul I must repent, or be damned forever!

How often have you bargained to sell your Saviour for less than thirty pieces of silver! Nay, for the merest trifle!

Finally, God wants volunteers to help on this great work. God has given Himself, and given His Son, and sent His Spirit; but more labourers still are needed; and what will you give? Paul said, I bear in my body the marks of the Lord Jesus. Do you aspire to such an honour? What will you do—what will you suffer? Say not, I have nothing to give. You can give yourself—your eyes, your ears, your hands, your mind, your heart, all; and surely nothing you have is too sacred and too good to be devoted to such a work upon such a call! How many young men are ready to go? and how many young women? Whose heart leaps up, crying, Here am I! send me?

2

THE WAGES OF SIN

"The wages of sin is death."—*Romans* 6 : 23.

THE death here spoken of is that which is due as the penal sanction of God's law.

In presenting the subject of our text, I must—

I. Illustrate the nature of sin ;

II. Specify some of the attributes of the penal sanctions of God's law ;

III. Show what this penalty must be.

I. An illustration will give us the best practical view of the nature of sin. You have only to suppose a government established to secure the highest well-being of the governed, and of the ruling authorities also. Supposed the head of this government to embark all his attributes in the enterprise—all his wealth, all his time, all his energies—to compass the high end of the highest general good. For this purpose he enacts the best possible laws—laws which, if obeyed, will secure the highest good of both subject and Prince. He then takes care to affix adequate penalties ; else all his care and wisdom must come to naught. He devotes to the interests of his government all he is and all he has, without reserve or abatement.

But some of his subjects refuse to sympathize with this movement. They say, "Charity begins at home," and they are for taking care of themselves in the first place ; in short, they are thoroughly selfish.

It is easy to see what this would be in a human government. The man who does this becomes the common enemy of the government and of all its subjects. *This is sin.* This illustrates precisely the case of the sinner. Sin is selfishness, It sets up a selfish end, and to gain it uses selfish means ; so that in respect to both its end and its means, it is precisely opposed to God and to all the ends of general happiness which he seeks to secure. It denies God's rights ; discards God's interests. Each sinner maintains that his own will shall be the law. The interest he sets himself to secure is entirely opposed to that proposed by God in His government.

All law must have sanctions. Without sanctions it would be only advice. It is therefore essential to the distinctive and inherent nature of law that it have sanctions.

These are either remuneratory or vindicatory. They promise reward for obedience, and they also threaten penalty for disobedience. They are vindicatory, inasmuch as they vindicate the honour of the violated law.

Again, sanctions may be either natural or governmental. Often both forms exist in other governments than the divine.

Natural penalties are those evil consequences which naturally result without any direct interference of government to punish. Thus in all governments the disrespect of its friends falls as a natural penalty on transgressors. They are the natural enemies of all good subjects.

In the divine government, compunctions of conscience and remorse fall into this class, and indeed many other things which naturally result to obedience on the one hand and to disobedience on the other.

There should also be governmental sanctions. Every governor should manifest his displeasure against the violation of his laws. To leave the whole question of obedience to mere natural consequences is obviously unjust to society.

Inasmuch as governments are established to sustain law and secure obedience, they are bound to put forth their utmost energies in this work.

Another incidental agency of government under some circumstances is that which we call discipline. One object of discipline is to go before the infliction of penalty, and force open unwilling eyes, to see that law has a government to back it up, and the sinner a fearful penalty to fear. Coming upon men during their probation, while as yet they have not seen or felt the fearfulness of penalty, it is designed to admonish them—to make them think and consider. Thus its special object is the good of the subject on whom it falls and of those who may witness its administration. It does not propose to sustain the dignity of law by exemplary inflictions. This belongs exclusively to the province of penalty. Discipline, therefore, is not penal in the sense of visiting crime with deserved punishment, but aims to dissuade the subject of law from violating its precepts.

Disciplinary agency could scarcely exist under a government of pure law, for the reason that such a government cannot defer the infliction of penalty. Discipline presupposes a state of suspended penalty. Hence penal inflictions must be broadly distinguished from disciplinary.

We are sinners, and therefore have little occasion to dwell on the remuneratory features of God's government. We can have no claim to remuneration under law, being precluded utterly by our sin. But with the penal features we have everything to do. I therefore proceed to enquire.

II. What are the attributes of the penal sanctions of God's law?

God has given us reason. This affirms intuitively and irresistibly all the great truths of moral government. There are certain attributes which we know must belong to the moral law, *e.g.*, one is *intrinsic justice*. Penalty should threaten no more and no less than is just.—Justice must be an attribute of God's law; else the whole universe must inevitably condemn it.

Intrinsic justice means and implies that the penalty be equal to the obligation violated. The guilt of sin consists in its being a violation of obligation. Hence the guilt must be in proportion to the magnitude of the obligation violated, and consequently the penalty must be measured by this obligation.

Governmental justice is another attribute. This feature of law seeks to afford security against transgression. Law is not governmentally just unless its penalty be so graduated as to afford the highest security against sin which the nature of the case admits. Suppose under any government the sanctions of law are trifling, not at all proportioned to the end to be secured. Snch a government is unjust to itself, and to the interests it is committed to maintain. Hence a good government must be governmentally just, affording in the severity of its penalties and the certainty of their just infliction, the highest security that its law shall be obeyed.

Again, penal sanctions should be worthy of the end aimed at by the law and by its author. Government is only a means to an end, this proposed end being universal obedience and its consequent happiness. If law is indispensable for obtaining this end, its penalty should be graduated accordingly.

Hence the penalty should be graduated by the importance of the precept. If the precept be of fundamental importance—of such importance that disobedience to it saps the very existence of all government—then it should be guarded by the greatest and most solemn sanctions. The penalties attached to its violation should be of the highest order.

Penalty should make an adequate expression of the lawgiver's views of the value of the end he proposes to secure by law; also of his views of the sacredness of his law; also of the intrinsic guilt of disobedience. Penalty aims to bring forth the *heart* of the lawgiver—to show the earnestness of his desire to maintain the right, and to secure that order and well-being which depend on obedience. In the greatness of the penalty the lawgiver brings forth his heart and pours the whole influence of his character upon his subjects.

The object of executing penalty is precisely the same ; not to gratify revenge, as some seem to suppose, but to act on the subjects of government with influences toward obedience. It has the same general object as the law itself has.

Penal sanctions should be an adequate expression of the lawgiver's regard for the public good and of his interest in it. In the precept he gave some expression ; in the penalty, he gives yet more. In the precept we see the object in view and have a manifestation of regard for the public interests ; in the penalty, we have a *measure* of this regard, showing us how *great* it is. For example, suppose a human law were to punish murder with only a trifling penalty. Under the pretence of being very tender-hearted, the lawgiver amerces this crime of murder with a fine of fifty cents ! Would this show that he greatly loved his subjects and highly valued their life and interests ? Far from it. You cannot feel that a legislator has done his duty unless he shows how much he values human life, and unless he attaches a penalty commensurate in some good degree with the end to be secured.

One word as to the infliction of capital punishment in human governments. There is a difference of opinion as to which is most effective, solitary punishment for life, or death. Leaving this question without remark, I have it to say that no man ever doubted that *the murderer deserves to die.* If some other punishment than death is to be preferred, it is not by any means because the murderer does not deserve death. No man can doubt this for a moment. It is one of the unalterable principles of righteousness, that if a man sacrifices the interest of another, he sacrifices his own ; an eye for an eye ; life for life.

We cannot but affirm that no government lays sufficient stress on the protection of human life unless it guards this trust with its highest penalties. Where life and all its vital interests are at stake, there the penalty should be great and solemn as is possible.

Moral agents have two sides to their sensibility; hope and fear;—to which you may address the prospect of good and the dread of evil. I am now speaking of penalty. This is addressed only to fear.

I have said in substance that penalty should adequately assert and vindicate the rightful authority of the lawgiver; should afford if possible an adequate rebuke of sin and should be based on a just appreciation of its nature. God's moral government embraces the whole intelligent universe, and stretches with its vast results onward through eternity. Hence the sweep and breadth of its interests are absolutely unlimited, and consequently the penalties of its law, being set to vindicate the authority of this government and to sustain these immeasurable interests, should be beyond measure dreadful. If anything beyond and more dreadful than the threatened penalty could be conceived, all minds would say—" This is not enough." With any just views of the relations and the guilt of sin, they could not be satisfied unless the penalty is the greatest that is conceivable. Sin is so vile, so mischievous, so terribly destructive and so far-sweeping in its ruin, moral agents could not feel that enough is done so long as more can be.

III. What is the penalty of God's moral law ?

Our text answers, " *death.*" This certainly is·not *animal death,* for saints die and animals also, neither of whom can be receiving the wages of sin. Besides, this would be no penalty if, after its infliction, men went at once to heaven. Such a penalty, considered as the wages of sin, would only be an insult to God's government.

Again, it cannot be *spiritual death,* for this is nothing else than a state of entire disobedience to the law. You cannot well conceive anything more absurb than to punish a man for disobedience by subjecting him to perpetual disobedience—an effort to sustain the law by dooming such offenders to its perpetual violation—and nothing more.

But this death *is* endless misery, corresponding to the death-penalty in human governments. Everybody knows what this is. It separates the criminal from society forever ; debars him at once and utterly from all the privileges of the government, and consigns him over to hopeless ruin. Nothing more dreadful can be inflicted. It is the extreme penalty, fearful beyond any other that is possible for man to inflict.

There can be no doubt that death as spoken of in our text is intended to correspond to the death-penalty in human governments.

You will also observe that in our text the " gift of God " which is " eternal life through Jesus Christ our Lord," is directly contrasted with death, the wages of sin. This fact may throw light on the question respecting the nature of this death. We must look for the antithesis of " *eternal life*."

Now this eternal life is not merely an eternal existence. Eternal life never means merely an eternal existence, in any case where it is used in Scripture ; but it does mean a state of eternal blessedness, implyng eternal holiness as its foundation. The use of the term " life " in Scripture in the sense of *real life*—a life worth living—*i.e.*, real and rich enjoyment, is so common as to supersede the necessity of special proof.

The penalty of death is therefore the opposite of this—viz., eternal misery.

I must here say a few words upon the *objections* raised against this doctrine of eternal punishment.

All the objections I have ever heard amount only to this,

that it is unjust. They may be expressed in somewhat various phraseology, but this is the only idea which they involve, of any moment at all.

(1.) It is claimed to be unjust because " life is so short."

How strangely men talk! Life so short, men have not time to sin enough to deserve eternal death! Do men forget that *one sin* incurs the penalty due for sinning? How many sins ought it to take to make one transgression of the law of God? Men often talk as if they supposed it must require a great many. As if a man must commit a great many murders before he has made up the crime of murder enough to fall under the sentence of the court! What? shall a man come before the court and plead that although he has broken the law to be sure, yet he has not lived long enough, and has not broken the law times enough, to incur its penalty? What court on earth ever recognized such a plea as proving any other than the folly and guilt of him who made it?

(2.) It is also urged that "man is so small, so very insignificant a being that he cannot possibly commit an infinite sin." What does this objection mean? Does it mean that sin is an act of creation, and to be measured therefore by the magnitude of that *something* which it creates? This would be an exceedingly wild idea of the nature of sin. Does the objection mean that man cannot violate an obligation of infinite strength? Then his meaning is simply *false,* as everybody must know. Does he imply that the guilt of sin is not to be measured by the obligation violated? Then he knows not what he says, or wickedly denies known truth. What? man so little that he cannot commit much sin! Is this the way we reason in analogous cases? Suppose your child disobeys you. He is very much smaller than you are! But do you therefore exonerate him from blame? Is this a reason which nullifies his guilt? Can no sin be committed by inferiors against their superior? Have sensible men always been mistaken in supposing that the younger and smaller are sometimes under obligations to obey the older and the greater ? Suppose you smite down the magistrate ; suppose you insult, or attempt to assassinate the king ; is this a very small crime, almost too excusable to be deemed a crime at all, because forsooth, you are in a lower position and he in a higher ? You say, " I am so little, so very insignificant ! How can I deserve so great a punishment ? " Do you reason so in any other case except your own sins against God ? Never.

(3.) Again, some men say, " Sin is not an infinite evil." This language is ambiguous. Does it mean that sin would not work infinite mischief if suffered to run on indefinitely ? This is false, for if only one soul were ruined by it, the mischief accruing from it would be infinite. Does it mean that sin is not an infinite evil, as seen in its present results and relations ? Suppose this admitted ; it proves nothing to our purpose, for it may be true that the sum total of evil results from each single sin will not all be brought out in any duration less than eternity. How then can you measure the evil of sin by what you see to-day ?

But there are still other considerations to show that the penalty of the law must be infinite. Sin is an infinite *natural* evil. It is so in this sense, that there are no bounds to the natural evil it would introduce if not governmentally restrained.

If sin were to ruin but one soul, there could be no limit set to the evil it would thus occasion.

Again, sin involves infinite guilt, for it is a violation of infinite obligation. Here it is important to notice a common mistake, growing out of confusion of ideas about the ground of obligation. From this, result mistakes in regard to what constitutes the guilt of sin. Here I might show that when you misapprehend the ground of obligation, you will almost of necessity misconceive the nature and extent of sin and guilt. Let us recur to our former illustration. Here is a government, wisely framed to secure the highest good of the governed and of all concerned. Whence arises the obligation to obey ? Certainly from the intrinsic value of the end sought to be secured. But how broad is this obligation to obey ; or, in other words, what is its true measure ? I answer, it exactly equals the value of the end which the government seeks to secure, and which obedience will secure, but which sin will destroy. By this measure of God the penalty must be graduated. By this the lawgiver must determine how much sanction, remuneratory and vindicatory, he must attach to his law in order to meet the demands of justice and benevolence.

Now God's law aims to secure the highest universal good. Its chief and ultimate end is not, strictly speaking, to secure supreme homage to God, but rather to secure the highest good of all intelligent moral beings — God, and all His creatures. So viewed, you will see that the intrinsic value of the end to be sought is the real ground of obligation to obey the precept. The value of this end being estimated, you have the value and strength of the obligation.

This is plainly infinite in the sense of being unlimited. In this sense we affirm obligation to be without limit. The very reason why we affirm any obligation at all is that the law is good and is the necessary means of the highest good of the universe. Hence the reason why we affirm any penalty at all compels us to affirm the justice and necessity of an infinite penalty. We see that intrinsic justice must demand an infinite penalty for the same reason that it demands any penalty whatever. If *any* penalty be just, it is just because law secures a certain good. If this good aimed at by the law be unlimited in extent, so must be the penalty. Governmental justice thus requires endless punishment ; else it provides no sufficient guaranty for the public good.

Again, the law not only *designs* but *tends to secure* infinite good. Its tendencies are direct to this end.—Hence its penalty should be infinite. The law is not just to the interests it both aims and tends to secure unless it arms itself with infinite sanctions.

Nothing less than infinite penalty can be an adequate expression of God's view of the value of the great end on which His heart is set. When men talk about eternal death being too great a penalty for sin, what do they think of God's efforts to restrain sin all over the moral universe ? What do they think of the death of His well-beloved Son ? Do they suppose it possible that God could give an adequate or a corresponding expression to His hatred of sin by any penalty less than endless ?

Nothing less could give an adequate expression to His regard for the authority of law. O, how fearful the results and how shocking the very idea, if God should fail to make an adequate expression of His regard for the sacredness of that law which underlies the entire weal of all His vast kingdom ?

You would insist that He shall regard the violation of His law as Universalists do. How surely he would bring down an avalanche of ruin on all His intelligent creatures if He were to yield to your demands ! Were He to affix anything less than endless penalty to His law, what holy being could trust the administration of His government !

His regard to the public good forbids His attaching a light or finite penalty to His law. He loves His subjects too well. Some people have strange notions of the way in which a ruler should express his regard for his subjects. They would have him so tender-hearted toward the guilty that they should absorb his entire sympathy and regard. They would allow him perhaps to fix a penalty of sixpence fine for the crime of murder, but not much if anything more. The poor murderer's wife and children are so precious you must not take away much of his money, and as to touching his liberty or his life—neither of these is to be thought of. What! do you not know that human nature is very frail and temptable, and therefore you ought to deal very sparingly with penalties for murder? Perhaps they would say, you may punish the murderer by keeping him awake one night—just one, no more; and God may let a guilty man's conscience disturb him about to this extent for the crime of murder! The Universalists do tell us that they will allow the most High God to give a man conscience that shall trouble him a little if he commits murder—a little, say for the first and perhaps the second offence; but they are not wont to notice the fact that under this penalty of a troubling conscience, the more a man sins, the less he has to suffer. Under the operation of this descending scale, it will soon come to this that a murderer would not get so much penalty as the loss of one night's sleep. But such are the notions that men reach when they swing clear of the affirmations of an upright reason and of God's revealing Word.

Speaking now to those who have a moral sense to affirm the right as well as eyes to see the operation of law, I know you cannot deny the logical necessity of the death-penalty for the moral law of God. There is a logical clinch to every one of these propositions which you cannot escape.

No penalty less than infinite and endless can be an adequate expression of God's displeasure against sin and of His determination to resist and punish it. The penalty should run on as long as there are subjects to be affected by it—as long as there is need of any demonstration of God's feelings and governmental course toward sin.

Nothing less is the greatest God can inflict, for He certainly can inflict an endless and infinite punishment. If therefore the exigency demands the greatest penalty He can inflict, this must be the penalty—*banishment from God and endless death.*

But I must pass to remark that the Gospel everywhere

assumes the same. It holds that by the deeds of the law no flesh can be justified before God. Indeed, it not only affirms this, but builds its entire system of atonement and grace upon this foundation. It constantly assumes that there is no such thing as paying the debt and canceling obligation ; and therefore that the sinner's only relief is forgiveness through redeeming blood.

Yet again, if the penalty be not endless death, *what is it*? Is it temporary suffering? Then how long does it last? When does it end? Has any sinner ever got through ; served out his time and been taken to heaven? We have no testimony to prove such a case, not the first one ; but we have the solemn testimony of Jesus Christ to prove that there never can be such a case. He tells us that there can be no passing from hell to heaven or from heaven to hell. A great gulf is fixed between, over which none shall ever pass. You may pass from earth to heaven, or from earth to hell ; but these two states of the future world are wide extremes, and no man or angel shall pass the gulf that divides them.

But you answer my question—What is the penalty? by the reply—It is only the natural consequences of sin as developed in a troubled conscience. Then it follows that the more a man sins the less he is punished, until it amounts to an infinitesimal quantity of punishment, for which the sinner cares just nothing at all. Who can believe this? Under this system, if a man fears punishment, he has only to pitch into sinning with the more will and energy ; he will have the comfort of feeling that he can very soon get over all his compunctions, and get beyond any penalty whatever! And do you believe this is God's only punishment for sin? You cannot believe it.

Universalists always confound discipline with penal sanctions. They overlook this fundamental distinction and regard all that men suffer here in this world as only penal. Whereas it is scarcely penal at all, but is chiefly disciplinary. They ask, What good will it do a sinner to send him to an endless hell? Is not God perfectly benevolent; and if so, how can He have any other object than to do the sinner all the good He can?

I reply, Punishment is not designed to do good to that sinner who is punished. It looks to other, remoter, and far greater good. Discipline, while he was on earth, sought mainly *his* personal good; penalty looks to other results. If you ask, Does not God aim to do good to the universal public by penalty? I answer, Even so; that is precisely what He aims to do.

Under human governments, the penalty may aim in part to reclaim. So far, it is discipline. But the death-penalty— after all suspension is past and the fatal blow comes, aims not to reclaim, and is not discipline, but is only penalty. The guilty man is laid on the great public altar and made a sacrifice for the public good. The object is to make a fearful, terrible impression on the public mind of the evil of transgression and the fearfulness of its consequences. Discipline looks not so much to the support of law as to the recovery of the offender. But the day of judgment has nothing to do with reclaiming the lost sinner. That and all its issues are purely penal. It is strange that these obvious facts should be overlooked.

There is yet another consideration often disregarded, viz., that, underlying any safe dispensation of discipline, there must be a moral law, sustained by ample and fearful sanctions, to preserve the law-giver's authority and sustain the majesty and honour of his government. It would not be safe to trust a system of discipline, and indeed it could not be expected to take hold of the ruined with much force, if it were not sustained by a system of law and penalty. This penal visitation on the unreclaimed sinner must stand forever, an appalling fact, to show that justice is realized, law vindicated, God honoured; and to make an enduring and awful impression of the evil of sin and of God's eternal hostility against it.

CONCLUSION

We hear a great many cavils against future punishment. At these we should not so much wonder, but for the fact that the Gospel assumes this truth, and then proposes a remedy. One would naturally suppose the mind would shrink ,from those fearful conclusions to which it is pressed when the relations of mere laws are contemplated ; but when the Gospel interposes to save, then it becomes passing strange that men should admit the reality of the Gospel, and yet reject the law and its penalties. They talk of *grace*; but what do they mean by grace ? When men deny the fact of sin, there is no room and no occasion for grace in the Gospel. Admitting nominally the fact of sin, but virtually denying its guilt, grace is only a name. Repudiating the sanctions of the law of God, and labouring to disprove their reality, what right have men to claim that they respect the Gospel ? They make it only a farce—or at least a system of *amends* for unreasonably severe legislation under the legal economy. Let not men who so traduce the law assume that they honour God by applauding His Gospel !

The representations of the Bible with regard to the final doom of the wicked are exceedingly striking. Spiritual truths are revealed by natural objects : *e.g.*, the gates and walls of the New Jerusalem, to present the splendours and glories of the heavenly state. A spiritual telescope is put into our hands ; we are permitted to point it towards the glorious city "whose builder and Maker is God;" we may survey its inner sanctuary, where the worshipping hosts praise God without ceasing. We see their flowing robes of white—the palms of victory in their hands—ths beaming joy of their faces—the manifestations of ineffable bliss in their souls. This is heaven pourtrayed in symbol. Who supposes that this is intended as hyperbole ? Who arraigns these representations as extravagant in speech, as if designed to overrate the case, or raise unwarrantable expectations? No man believes this. No man ever brings this charge against what the Bible says of heaven. What is the object in adopting this figurative mode of representation? Beyond question, the object is to give the best possible conception of the facts.

Then we have the other side. The veil is lifted, and you come to the very verge of hell to see what is there. Whereas on the one hand all was glorious, on the other all is fearful, and full of horrors.

There is a bottomless pit. A deathless soul is cast therein; it sinks and sinks and sinks, going down that awful pit which knows no bottom, weeping and wailing as it descends, and you hear its groans as they echo and re-echo from the sides of that dread cavern of woe!

Here is another image. You have a "lake of fire and brimstone," and you see lost sinners thrown into its waves of rolling fire; and they lash its burning shore, and gnaw their tongues for pain. There the worm dieth not, and their fire is not quenched, and "not one drop of water" can reach them to "cool their tongues"—"tormented in that flame."

What think you? Has God said these things to frighten our poor souls? Did He mean to play on our fears for His own amusement? Can you think so? Nay, does it not rather grieve His heart that He must build such a hell, and *must* plunge therein the sinners who will not honour His law—will not embrace salvation from sinning. through His grace? Ah, the waves of death roll darkly under the eye of the Holy and compassionate One! He has no pleasure in the death of the sinner! But He must sustain His throne, and save His loyal subjects if He can.

Turn to another scene. Here is a death-bed. Did you ever see a sinner die? Can you describe the scene? Was it a friend, a relative, dear, very dear to your heart? How long was he dying? Did it seem to you the death-agony would never end? When my last child died, the struggle was long; O, it was fearfully protracted and agonizing! Twenty-four hours in the agonies of dissolving nature! It made me sick; I could not see it! But suppose it had continued till this time. I should long since have died myself under the anguish and nervous exhaustion of witnessing such a scene. So would all our friends. Who could survive to the final termination of such an awful death? Who would not cry out—"My God, cut it short, cut it short in mercy!" When my wife died, her death-struggles were long and heart-rending. If you had been there, you would have cried mightily to God—"Cut it short! O, cut it short and relieve this dreadful agony! But suppose it had continued, on and on, by day and by night— day after day, through its slow moving hours, and night after night—*long* nights, as if there could be no morning. The figure of our text supposes an eternal dying. Let us conceive such a case. Suppose it should actually occur in some dear circle of sympathizing friends. A poor man cannot die! He lingers in the death-agony a month, a year, five years, ten years—till all his friends are broken down, and fall into their graves under the insupportable horror of the scene: but still the poor man cannot die! He outlives one generation—then another and another; one hundred years he is dying in mortal agony, and yet he comes no nearer to the end! What would you think of such a scene? It would be an illustration—that is all—a feeble illustration of the awful "*second death !*"

God would have us understand what an awful thing sin is, and what fearful punishment it deserves. He would fain show us by such figures how terrible must be the doom of the determined sinner. Did you ever see a sinner die? and did you not cry out—Surely the curse of God has fallen heavily on this world! Ah, this is only a faint emblem of that heavier curse that comes in the "*second death !*"

The text affirms that death is the "wages of sin." It is just what sin deserves. Labour earns wages, and creates a rightful claim to such remuneration. So men are conceived as earning wages when they sin. They become entitled to their pay. God deems Himself holden to give them their well-deserved wages.

As I have often said, I would not say one word in this direction to distress your souls, if there were no hope and no mercy possible. Would I torment you before the time? God forbid! Would I hold out the awful penalty before you, and tell you there is no hope? No. I say these things to make you feel the need of escaping for your life.

Think of this: "the wages of sin is death!" God is aiming to erect a monument that shall proclaim to all the universe—*Stand in awe and sin not!* So that whenever they shall look on this awful expression, they shall say—What an awful thing sin is! People are wont to exclaim—O, how horrible the *penalty!* They are but too apt to overlook the horrible *guilt* and *ill-desert* of sin! When God lays a sinner on his death-bed before our eyes, He invites us to look at the *penalty of sin.* There he lies, agonizing, groaning, quivering, racked with pain, yet he lives, and lives on. Suppose he lives on in this dying state a day, a week, a month, a year, a score of years, a century, a thousand years, a thousand ages, and still he lives on, "dying perpetually, yet never dead:" finally, the universe passes away; the heavens are rolled together as a scroll—and what then? There lies that sufferer yet. He looks up and cries out, "*How long*, O HOW LONG?" Like the knell of eternal death, the answer comes down to him, "*Eternally*, ETERNALLY." Another cycle of eternal ages rolls on, and again he dares to ask, *how long?* and again the answer rolls back—"*Eternally*, ETERNALLY!" O how this fearful answer comes down thundering through all the realms of agony and despair!

We are informed that in the final consummation of earthly

scenes, "the judgment shall sit and the books shall be opened." We shall be there, and what is more, *there* to close up our account with our Lord and receive our allotment. Which will you have on that final settlement day? The wages of sin? Do you say, "Give me my wages—give me my wages; I will not be indebted to Christ?" Sinner, you shall have them. God will pay you without fail or stint. He has made all the necessary arrangements, and has your wages ready. But take care what you do! Look again before you take your final leap. Soon the curtain will fall, probation close, and all hope will have perished. Where then shall I be? And you, *where?* On the right hand or on the left?

The Bible locates hell in the sight of heaven. The smoke of their torment as it rises up forever and ever, is in full view from the heights of the Heavenly City. There, you adore and worship; but as you cast your eye afar off toward where the rich man lay, you see what it costs to sin. There, not one drop of water can go to cool their burning tongues. Thence the smoke of their torment rises and rises for evermore! Take care what you do to-day!

Suppose you are looking into a vast crater, where the surges of molten lava boil and roll up, and roll and swell, and ever and anon belch forth huge masses to deluge the plains below. Once in my life, I stood in sight of Etna, and dropped my eye down into its awful mouth. I could not forbear to cry out "*tremendous*, TREMENDOUS!" There, said I, is an image of hell! O, sinner, think of *hell*, and of yourself thrust into it. It pours forth its volumes of smoke and flame forever, never ceasing, never exhausted. Upon that spectacle the universe can look and read—"The wages of sin is death! O, sin not, since such is the doom of the unpardoned sinner!" Think what a demonstration this is in the government of God! What an exhibition of His holy justice, of His inflexible purpose to sustain the interests of holiness and happiness in all His vast dominions! Is not this worthy of God, and of the sacredness of His great scheme of moral government?

Sinner, you may now escape this fearful doom. This is the reason why God has revealed hell in His faithful Word. And now shall this revelation, to you, be in vain and worse than in vain?

What would you think if this whole congregation were pressed by some resistless force close up to the very brink of hell : but just as it seemed that we are all to be pushed over the awful brink, an angel rushes in, shouting as with seraphic trump, "*Salvation is possible—Glory to God*, GLORY TO GOD, GLORY TO GOD!"

You cry aloud—Is it possible? Yes, yes, he cries, let me take you up in my broad, loving arms, and bear you to the feet of Jesus, for He is mighty and willing to save!

Is all this mere talk? Oh, if I could wet my lips with the dews of heaven, and bathe my tongue in its founts of eloquence, even then I could not describe the realities.

Christian people, are you figuring round and round to get a little property, yet neglecting souls? Beware, lest you ruin souls that can never live again! Do you say—I thought they knew it all? They reply to you—"I did not suppose you believed a word of it yourselves. You did not act as if you did. Are you going to heaven? Well, I am going down to hell! There is no help for me now. You will sometimes think of me then, as you shall see the smoke of my woe rising up darkly athwart the glorious heavens. After I have been there a long, long time, you will sometimes think that I, who once lived by your side, am there. O remember, you cannot pray for me then ; but you will remember that once you might have warned and might have saved me."

O methinks, if there can be bitterness in heaven, it must enter through such an avenue and spoil your happiness there!

3

THE EXCUSES OF SINNERS

"Wilt thou also disannul my judgment? Wilt thou condemn me, that thou mayest be righteous?"—*Job* xl. 8.

ALTHOUGH in the main, Job had spoken correctly of God, yet in his great anguish and perturbation under his sore trials, he had said some things which were hasty and abusive. For these the Lord rebuked him. This rebuke is contained in our context:

"Moreover the Lord answered Job, and said—Shall he that contendeth with the Almighty instruct Him? He that reproveth God, let him answer it.

"Then Job answered the Lord, and said—Behold I am vile; what shall I answer thee? I will lay my hand upon my mouth. Once have I spoken, but I will not answer; yea, twice, but I will proceed no further.

"Then answered the Lord unto Job out of the whirlwind, and said—Gird up thy loins now like a man; I will demand of thee, and declare thou unto me. Wilt thou also disannul my judgment? Wilt thou condemn me, that thou mayest be righteous?"—*Job* xl. 1—8.

It is not, however, my object to discuss the original purpose and connection of these words, but rather to consider their present application to the case of sinners. In pursuing this object, I shall

I. Show that every excuse for sin condemns God.

II. Consider some of these excuses in detail.

III. Show that excuse for sin adds insult to injury.

I. *Every excuse for sin condemns God.* This will be apparent if we consider,

1. *That nothing can be sin for which there is a justifiable excuse.*

This is entirely self-evident. It therefore needs neither elucidation nor proof.

2. *If God condemns that for which there is a good excuse, He must be wrong.* This also is self-evident. If God condemns what we have good reason for doing, no intelligence in the universe can justify Him.

3. *But God does condemn all sin.* He condemns it utterly, and will not allow the least apology or excuse for it. Hence, either there is no apology for it, or God is wrong.

4. Consequently, *every excuse for sin charges blame upon God,* and virtually accuses Him of tyranny. Whoever pleads an excuse for sin, therefore, charges God with blame.

II. We will consider some of these excuses, and see whether the principles I have laid down are not just and true.

1. INABILITY. No excuse is more common. It is echoed and re-echoed over every Christian land, and handed down age after age, never to be forgotten. With unblushing face it is proclaimed that men *cannot* do what God requires of them.

Let us examine this and see what it amounts to. God, it is said, requires what men cannot do. And does He *know* that men cannot do it? Most certainly. Then He has no apology for requiring it, and the requisition is most unreasonable. Human reason can never justify it. It is a natural impossibility.

But again, *upon what penalty* does God require what man cannot do? The threatened penalty is eternal death! Yes, *eternal death,* according to the views of those who plead inability as an excuse. God requires me, on pain of eternal death, to do that which He knows I cannot do. Truly this condemns God in the worst sense. You might just as well charge God outright with being an infinite tyrant.

Moreover, it is not for us to say whether on these conditions we shall or shall not charge God with infinite tyranny, for we cannot help it. The law of our reason demands it.

Hence, those who plant themselves upon these grounds charge God with infinite tyranny. Perhaps, sinner, you little think when you urge the excuse of inability, that you are really arraigning God on the charge of infinite tyranny. And you, Christian, who make this dogma of inability a part of your "orthodox" creed, may have little noticed its blasphemous bearings against the character of God; but your failure to notice it alters not the fact. The black charge is involved in the very doctrine of inability, and cannot be explained out of it.

I have intimated that this charge is blasphemous against God—and most truly. Far be it from God to do any such thing! Shall God require natural impossibilities, and denounce eternal death upon men for not doing what they have no natural power to do? Never! Yet good men and bad men agree together to charge God with doing this very thing, and doing it not once or twice only, but uniformly through all ages, with all the race, from the beginning to the end of time! Horrible! Nothing in all the government of God ever so insulted and abused Jehovah! Nothing was ever more blasphemous and false! God says, "his commandments are not grievous;" but you, by this excuse of inability, proclaim that God's words are false. You declare that His commands are not only grievous, but are even *naturally impossible!* Hark! what does the Lord Jesus say? "My yoke is easy and my burden is light." And do you deny this? Do you rise up in the very face of His words and say—"Lord, Thy yoke is so hard that no man can possibly endure it; Thy burden is so heavy that no man can ever bear it?" Is not this gainsaying and blaspheming Him who can not lie?

But you take the ground that no man can obey the law of God. As the Presbyterian Confession of Faith has it, "No man is able, either by himself, or by any grace received in this life, perfectly to keep the commandments of God; but doth daily break them in thought, word, and deed." Observe, this affirms not only that no man is naturally able to keep God's commands, but also that no man is able to do it *"by any grace received in this life;"* thus making this declaration a libel on the Gospel as well as a palpable misrepresentation of the law of its Author, and of man's relations to both. It is only moderate language to call this assertion from the Confession of Faith *a libel.* If there is a lie, either in hell or out of hell, *this is a lie,* or God is an infinite tyrant. If reason be allowed to speak at all, it is impossible for her to say less or otherwise than thus. And has not God constituted the reason of man for the very purpose of taking cognizance of the rectitude of all his ways?

Let God be true though every man be proved a liar! In the present case, the remarkable fact that no man can appease his own conscience and satisfy himself that he is truly unable to keep the law, shows that *man* lies, not God.

2. A second excuse which sinners make is *want of time.*

Suppose I tell one of my sons—" Go, do this or that duty, on pain of being whipped to death." He replies, "Father, I can't possibly do it, for I have not time. I must be doing that other business which you told me to do; and besides, if I had nothing else to do, I could not possibly do this new business in the time you allow." Now if this statement be the truth, and I knew it when I gave him the command, then I am a tyrant. There is no evading this charge. My conduct toward my son is downright tyranny.

So if God really requires of you what you have not time to do, He is infinitely to blame. For He surely knows how little time you have, and it is undeniable that He enforces His requisitions with most terrific penalties. What! is God so reckless of justice, so regardless of the well-being of His creatures, that He can sport with red-hot thunder-bolts, and hurl them, despite of justice and right, among His unfortunate creatures? *Never!* NEVER! This is not true; it is only the false assumption which the sinner makes when he pleads as his excuse, *that he has not time to do what God demands of him.*

Let me ask you, sinner, how much time will it take you to do the first great duty which God requires—namely, *give Him your heart?* How long will this take? How long need you be in making up your mind to serve and love God? Do you not know that this, when done, will be done in one moment of time? And how long need you be in persuading yourself to do it?

Your meaning may be this : Lord, it takes me so long to make up my mind to serve thee, it seems as if I never should get time enough for this ; even the whole of life seems almost too short for me to bring my mind to this unwelcome decision. Is this your meaning, sinner?

But let us look on all sides of the subject. Suppose I say to my son—"Do this now, my son ; " and he replies, "I can't, father, for I must do that other thing you told me to do." Does God do so? No. God only requires the duty of each moment in its time. This is all. He only asks us to use faithfully just all the power He has given us—nothing more. He only requires that we do the best we can. When He prescribes the amount of love which will please Him, He does not say—Thou shalt love the Lord thy God with the powers of an angel—with the burning heart of a seraph—no, but only " with all *thy heart* "—this is all. An infinitely ridiculous plea is this of the sinner's, that he can not do as well as he can—can not love God with all his own heart, and soul, and mind, and strength. Thou shalt do the best that thou art able to do, says God to the sinner. Ah, says the sinner, I am not able to do that. Oh, what stupid nonsense !

You charge that God is unreasonable. The truth is, God is the most reasonable of all beings. He asks only that we should use each moment for Him, in labour, or in rest, whichever is most for His glory. He only requires that with the

time, talents, and strength which He has given us, we should
do all we can to serve Him.

Says that mother—"How can I be religious? I have to
take care of all my children." Indeed! and can't you get
time to serve God? What does God require of you? That
you should forsake and neglect your children? No, indeed;
He asks you to take care of your children—good care of
them; and *do it all for God.* He says to you—Those are *my*
children; and He puts them into your hands, saying—Take
care of them for Me, and I will give thee wages. And now
will it require more time to take care of your children for God,
than to take care of them for yourself? O, but you say, I
cannot be religious, for I must be up in the morning and get
my breakfast. And how much longer will it take you to
get your breakfast ready to please God, than to do the
same to please yourself? How much longer time must
you have to do your duties religiously, than to do them
selfishly?

What, then, do you mean by this plea? The fact is, all
these excuses show that the excuser is mad—not insane, but
mad. For what does God require so great that you should
be unable to do it for want of time? Only this, that you
should do all *for God.* Persons who make this plea seem to
have entirely overlooked the real nature of religion, and of
the requisitions that God makes of them. So it is with the
plea of inability. The sinner says, "I am unable." Unable
to do what? Just what you can do; for God never requires
anything beyond this. Unless, therefore, you assume that
God requires of you more than you can do, your plea is false,
and even ridiculous. If, on the other hand, you do not
assume this, then your plea, if true, would not show God to
be unjust.

But I was saying that in this plea of having no time to be
religious, men entirely overlook or pervert the true idea of
religion. The farmer pleads—"I can't be religious; I can't

serve God—I must sow my wheat." Well, sow your wheat ; but do it *for the Lord*. O but you have *so much* to do ! Then do it all for the Lord. Another can't be religious for he must get his lesson. Well, get your lesson, but get it *for the Lord,* and this will be religious. The man who should neglect to sow his wheat or neglect to get his lessons because he wants to be religious, is crazy. He perverts the plainest things in the worst way. If you are to be religious, you must be industrious. The farmer must sow his wheat, and the student must get his lesson. An idle man can no more be religious than the devil can be. This notion that men can't be religious, because they have some business to do, is the merest nonsense. It utterly overlooks the great truth that God never forbids our doing the appropriate business of life, but only requires that we shall do all for Himself. If God did require us to serve Him in such a way as would compel us to neglect the practical duties of life, it would be truly a hard case. But now the whole truth is, that He requires us to do precisely these duties, and do them all honestly and faithfully *for Him,* and in the best possible manner. Let the farmer take care of his farm, and see that he does it well, and above all, do it *for God.* It is God's farm, and the heart of every farmer is God's heart, therefore let the farm be tilled for God, and the heart be devoted to *Him alone.*

3. Men plead *a sinful nature for their excuse.* And pray, what is this sinful nature ? Do you mean by it that every faculty and even the very essence of your constitution were poisoned and made sinful in Adam, and came down in this polluted state by inheritance to you ? Do you mean that you were so born in sin that the substance of your being is all saturated with it, and so that all the faculties of your constitution are themselves *sin ?* Do you believe this ?

I admit if this were true, it would make out a hard case. A hard case indeed ! Until the laws of my reason are changed, it would compel me to speak out openly and say—Lord, this

is a hard case, that Thou shouldst make my nature itself a
sinner, and then charge the guilt of its sin upon me! I could
not help saying this; the deep echoings of my inner being
would proclaim it without ceasing, and the breaking of ten
thousand thunderbolts over my head would not deter me from
thinking and saying so. The reason God has given me would
forever affirm it.

But the dogma is an utter absurdity. For, pray, what *is
sin?* God answers—" transgression of law." And now you
hold that your nature is itself a breach of the law of God—
nay, that it has always been a breach of God's law, from Adam
to the day of your birth; you hold that the current of this
sin came down in the veins and blood of your race—and *who
made it so?* Who created the veins and blood of man?
From whose hand sprang this physical constitution and this
mental constitution? Was man his own creator? Did sin
do a part of the work in creating your physical and your
mental constitution? Do you believe any such thing? No;
you ascribe your nature and its original faculties to God, and
upon Him, therefore, you charge the guilty authorship of your
" sinful nature."

But how strange a thing is this! If man is in fault for his
sinful nature, why not condemn man for having blue or black
eyes? The fact is, sin never can consist in having a nature,
nor in what nature *is;* but only and alone in the bad use
which we make of our nature. This is all. Our Maker will
never find fault with us for what He has Himself done or
made; certainly not. He will not condemn us, if we will only
make a right use of our powers—of our intellect, our sensibility, and our will. He never holds us responsible for our
original nature. If you will observe, you will find that God
has given no law prescribing what sort of nature and consti-
tutional powers we should have. He has given no law on
these points, the transgression of which, if given, might
somewhat resemble the definition of sin. But now since

there is no law about nature, nature cannot be a transgression.

Here let me say, that if God were to make a law prescribing what nature or constitution a man must have, it could not possible be otherwise than unjust and absurd, for the reason that man's nature is not a proper subject for legislation, precept, and penalty, inasmuch as it lies entirely without the pale of voluntary action, or of any action of man at all. And yet thousands of men have held the dogma that sin consists in great part in having a sinful nature. Yes, through long ages of past history, grave theologians have gravely taught this monstrous dogma ; it has resounded from pulpits, and has been stereotyped for the press, and men have seemed to be never weary of glorifying this dogma as the surest test of sound orthodoxy ! *Orthodoxy ! !* There never was a more infamous libel on Jehovah ! It would be hard to name another dogma which more violently outrages common sense. It is nonsense—absurd and utter NONSENSE ! I would to God that it were not even worse than nonsense ! Think what mischief it has wrought ! Think how it has scandalized the law, the government, and the character of God ! Think how it has filled the mouths of sinners with excuses from the day of its birth to this hour !

Now I do not mean to imply that the men who have held this dogma have intelligently insulted God with it. I do not imply that they have been aware of the impious and even blasphemous bearings of this dogma upon Jehovah ;—I am happy to think that some at least have done all this mischief ignorantly. But the blunder and the mischief have been none the less for the honest ignorance in which they were done.

4. Sinners, in self-excuse, say they *are willing to be Christians.* They are willing, they say, to be sanctified. O yes, they are very willing ; but there is some great difficulty lying further back or something else—perhaps they do

not know just where—but it is *somewhere,* and it will not let them become Christians.

Now the fact is, if we are really willing, there is nothing more which we can do. Willing is all we have to do *morally* in the case, and all we can do. But the plea, as in the sinner's mouth, maintains that God requires of us what is naturally impossible. It assumes that God requires of us something more than right willing ; and this, be it what it may, is, of course, to us, an impossibility. If I will to move my muscles, and no motion follows, I have done all I can do ; there is a difficulty beyond my reach, and I am in no blame for its exist-ence, or for its impediment. Just so, if I were to will to serve God, and absolutely no effect should follow, I have done my utmost, and God never can demand anything more. In fact, to will is the very thing which God does require. " If there be first a willing mind, it is accepted." Do tell me, parent, if you had told your child to do anything, and you saw him exerting himself to the utmost, would you ask anything more ? If you should see a parent demanding and enforcing of a child more than he could possibly do, however willing, would you not denounce that parent as a tyrant ? Certainly you would. The slave-driver, even, is not wont to beat his slave, if he sees him willing to do all he can.

This plea is utterly false, for no sinner is willing to be any better than he actually is. If the will is right, all is right ; and universally the state of the will is the measure of one's moral character. Those men, therefore, who plead that they are willing to be Christians while yet they remain in their sins, talk mere nonsense.

5. *Sinners say they are waiting God's time.* A lady in Philadelphia had been in great distress of mind for many years. On calling to see her, I asked—" What does God require of you ? What is your case ? " " Oh," said she, " God waited on me a long time before I began to seek Him at all, and now I must wait for Him as long as He did for me.

So my minister tells me. You see, therefore, that I am waiting in great distress for God to receive me."

Now what is the real meaning of this? 'It comes to this; God urges me to duty, but is not ready for me to do it; He tells me to come to the Gospel feast, and I am ready; but He is not ready to let me in.

Now does not this throw all the blame upon God? Could anything do so more completely than this does? The sinner says—"I am ready, and willing, and waiting; but God is not yet ready for me to stop sinning. His hour has not yet come.".

When I first began to preach, I found this notion almost universal. Often, after pressing men to duty, I have been accosted—"What, you throw all the blame upon the sinner!" "Yes, indeed I do," would be my reply. An old lady once met me after preaching and broke out, "What! you set men to getting religion themselves! You tell them to repent themselves? You don't mean *so*, do you?" "Indeed I *do*," said I. She had been teaching for many years that the sinner's chief duty is to await God's time.

6. Sinners plead in excuse, that *their circumstances are very peculiar*. I know my duty well enough, but my circumstances are so peculiar. And does not God understand your circumstances? Nay, has not His providence been concerned in making them what they are? If so, then you are throwing blame upon God. You say—"O Lord, Thou art a hard Master, for Thou hast never made any allowance for my circumstances."

But how much, sinner, do you really mean in making this plea? Do you mean that your circumstances are so peculiar that God ought to excuse you from becoming religious, at least for the present? If you do not mean as much as this, why do you make your circumstances your excuse at all? If you do mean this, then you are just as much mistaken as you can be. For God requires you, despite of your circumstances, to

abandon your sin. If, now, your circumstances are so peculiar
that you cannot serve God in them, you must abandon them
or lose your soul. If they are such as admit of your serving
God in them, then do so at once.

But you say—"I can't get out of my circumstances." I
reply, You can ; you can get out of the wickedness of them ;
for if it is necessary in order to serve God, you can change
them ; and if not, you can repent and serve God in them.

7. The sinner's next excuse is that *his temperament is
peculiar.* " Oh," he says, " I am very nervous ; or my temperament is very sluggish ; I seem to have no sensibility."
Now what does God require ? Does He require of you another
or a different sensibility from your own ? Or does He require
only that you should use what you have according to the law
of love ?

But such is the style of a multitude of excuses. One has
too little excitement ; another, too much ; so neither can
possibly repent and serve God ! A woman came to me, and
pleaded that she was naturally too excitable, and dared not
trust herself ; and therefore could not repent. Another
has the opposite trouble—too sluggish—scarce ever sheds a
tear—and therefore could make nothing out of religion if he
should try. But does God require you to shed more tears than
you are naturally able to shed ? Or does He only require
that you should serve Him ? Certainly this is all. Serve
Him with the very powers He has given you. Let your nerves
be ever so excitable, come and lay those quivering sensibilities
over into the hands of God—pour out that sensibility into the
heart of God !—this is all that He requires. I know how
to sympathize with that woman, for I know much about a
burning sensibility ; but does God require feeling and excitement ? Or only a perfect consecration of all our powers to
Himself ?

8. But, says another, my health is so poor that I can't go
to meeting, and therefore can't be religious.

Well, what does God require? Does He require that you should go to all the meetings, by evening or by day, whether you have the requisite health for it or not? Infinitely far from it. If you are not able to go to meeting, yet you can give God your heart. If you can not go in bad weather, be assured that God is infinitely the most reasonable being that ever existed. He makes all due allowance for every circumstance. Does He not know all your weakness? Indeed He does. And do you suppose that He comes into your sickroom and denounces you for not being able to go to meeting, or for not attempting when unable, and for not doing all in your sickness that you might do in health? No, not He; but He comes into your sick-room *as a Father*. He comes to pour out the deepest compassions of His heart in pity and in love; and why should you not respond to His loving-kindness? He comes to you and says—" Give me your heart, my child." And now you reply—" I have no heart." Then He has nothing to ask of you—*He thought you had;* and thought, too, that He had done enough to draw your heart in love and gratitude to Himself. He asks—"What can you find in all my dealings with you that is grievous? If nothing, why do you bring forward pleas in excuse for sin that accuse and condemn God?"

9. Another excuse is in this form—" *My heart is so hard, that I can not feel.*" This is very common, both among professors and non-professors. In reality it is only another form of the plea of inability. In fact, all the sinner's excuses amount only to this—" *I am unable*"—" I can't do what God requires." If the plea of a hard heart is any excuse at all, it must be on the ground of real inability.

But what *is* hardness of heart? Do you mean that you have so great apathy of the sensibility that you can not get up any emotion? Or, do you mean that you have no power to will or to act right? Now on this point, it should be considered that the emotions are altogether involuntary.

They go and come according to circumstances, and therefore are never required by the law of God, and are not, properly speaking, either religion itself, or any part of it. Hence, if by a hard heart you mean a dull sensibility, you mean what has no concern with the subject. God asks you to yield your will, and consecrate your affections to Himself, and He asks this, whether you have any feeling or not.

Real hardness of heart, in the Bible use of the phrase, means *stubbornness of will.* So in the child, a hard heart means a will set in fixed stubbornness against doing its parent's bidding. The child may have in connection with this, either much or little emotion. His sensibilities may be acute and thoroughly aroused, or they may be dormant ; and yet the stubborn will may be there in either case.

Now the hardness of heart of which God complains in the sinner is precisely of this sort. The sinner cleaves to his self-indulgence, and will not relinquish it, and then complains of hardness of heart. What would you think of a child, who, when required to do a most reasonable thing, should say— " My heart is so hard, I can't yield." " O," he says, " my will is so set to have my own way that I cannot possibly yield to my father's authority."

This complaint is extremely common. Many a sinner makes it, who has been often warned, often prayed with and wept over, who has been the subject of many convictions. And does he really mean by this plea that he finds his will so obstinate that he can not make up his mind to yield to God's claims ? Does he mean this, and does he intend really to publish his own shame ? Suppose you go to the devils in hell, and press on them the claims of God, and they should reply— " O, my heart is so hard, I can't"—what would be their meaning ? Only this : I am so obstinate—my will is so set in sin, that I can not for a moment indulge the thought of repentance. This would be their meaning, and if the sinner tells the truth of himself, and uses language correctly, he must mean the same. But oh, how does he add insult to injury by this declaration! Suppose a child should plead this—I can not find it in my heart to love my father and my mother ; my heart is so hard towards them ; I never can love them; I can feel pleasure only in abusing them, and trampling down their authority. *What a plea is this?* Does not this heap insult upon wrong? Or suppose a murderer arraigned before the court, and permitted before his sentence to speak, if he had ought to say why sentence should not be passed ;— suppose he should rise and say—" May it please the court, my heart for a long time has been as hard as a millstone. I have murdered so many men, and have been in the practice so long, that I can kill a man without the least compunction of conscience. Indeed, I have such an insatiable thirst for blood that I can not help murdering whenever I have a good oppor- tunity. In fact, my heart is so hard that I find I like this employment full as well as any other."

Well, how long will the court listen to such a plea? "Hold there! hold!" the judge would cry—"you infamous villain, we can hear no more such pleas! Here, sheriff, bring in a gallows, and hang the man within these very walls of justice, for I will not leave the bench until I see him dead! He will murder us all here in this house if he can!"

Now what shall we think of the sinner who says the same thing? O God, he says, my heart is so hard I never can love Thee. I hate Thee so sincerely I never can make up my mind to yield this heart to Thee in love and willing sub- mission!

Sinners, how many of you (in this house) have made this plea—"My heart is so hard, I can't repent. I can't love and serve God!" Go, write it down ; publish it to the universe— make your boast of being so hard-hearted that no claims of God can ever move you. Methinks if you were to make such a plea, you would not be half through before the whole universe would hiss you from their presence and chase you from the face of these heavens till you would cry out for some rocks or mountains to hide you from their scathing rebukes! Their voice of indignation would rise up and ring along the arch of heaven like the roar of ten thousand tornadoes, and whelm you with unutterable confusion and shame! What, do you insult and abuse the Great Jehovah? Oh! do you condemn that very God who has watched over you in unspeakable love—fanned you with His gentle zephyrs in your sickness—feasted you at His own table, and you would not thank Him, or even notice His providing hand? And then when the sympathy of your Christian friends has pressed you with entreaties to repent, and they have made you a special subject of their prayers—when angels have wept over you, and unseen spirits have lifted their warning voices in your pathway to hell—you turn up your face of brass towards Jehovah, and tell Him your heart is so hard you can't repent, and don't care whether you ever do or not! You seize a spear and plunge it into the heart of the crucified One, and then cry out—"I can't be sorry, not I; my heart is hard as a stone! I don't care, and I will not repent!" What a wretch you are, sinner, if this is your plea.

But what does your plea amount to? Only this—that your heart is fully set to do evil. The sacred writer has revealed your case most clearly—"Because vengeance against an evil work is not executed speedily, therefore the heart of the sons of men *is fully set* in them to do evil." You stand before the Lord just in this daring, blasphemous attitude—fully set in your heart *to do evil*.

10. Another form of the same plea is, *My heart is so wicked I can't.* Some do not hesitate to avow this wickedness of heart. What do they mean by it? Do they mean that they are so hardened in sin, and so desperately wicked, that they will not bow? This is the only proper sense of their language, and this is the precise truth.

Since you bring this forward, sinner, as your excuse, your object must be to charge this wickedness of heart upon God. Covertly, perhaps, but really, you imply that God is concerned in creating that wicked heart! This is it, and this is the whole of it. You would feel no interest in the excuse, and it would never escape your lips but for this tacit implication that God is in fault for your wicked heart. This is only the plea of inability, coupled with its twin sister, original sin, coming down in the created blood and veins of the race, under the Creator's responsibility.

11. Another kindred plea is—*My heart is so deceitful.* Suppose a man should make this excuse for deceiving his neighbour—" I can't help cheating you. I can't help lying to you and abusing you ; my heart is so deceitful ! " Would any man in his senses ever suppose that this could be an apology or excuse for doing wrong ? Never. Of course, unless the sinner means in this plea to set forth his own guilt and condemn himself, he must intend it as some sort of justification ; and, if so, he must, in just so far, cast the blame upon God. And this is usually his intention. He does not mean sincerely to confess his own guilt ; no, he charges the guilt of his deceitful heart upon God.

12. Another excuses himself by the plea, *I have tried to become a Christian.* I have done all I can do ; I have tried often, earnestly, and long.

You have tried, then, you say, to be a Christian ; what is being a Christian ? Giving your heart to God. And what is giving your heart to God ? Devoting your voluntary powers to Him ; ceasing to live for yourself and living for God. This is being a Christian—the state you profess to have been trying to attain.

No excuse is more common than this. And what is legitimately implied in this trying to be a Christian. A willingness to do your duty is always implied ; that the heart, that is, the *will* is *right* already ; and the trying refers only to the outward efforts—the executive acts. For there is no sense whatever in a man's saying that he is trying to do what he has no intention or will to do. The very statement implies that his will is not only in favour, but is thoroughly committed and really in earnest to attain the end chosen.

Consequently, if a man tries to be a Christian his heart is obedient to God, and his trying must respect his outward action. These are so connected with the will that they follow by a law of necessity unless the connection is broken ; and, when this takes place, no sin attends our failure to secure the outward act. God does not hold us responsible.

Hence, the sinner ought to mean by this plea—"I have obeyed God a long time"—I have had a right heart—and I have tried sincerely to secure such external action as comports with Christian character.

Now, if this be true, you have done your duty. But do you mean to affirm all this ? No, you say. Then what *do* you mean ?

Suppose I should say to my son, "Do this ; do it, my son ; why have you not done it ?" "O," he says, "father, I have *tried ;*" but he does not mean that he has ever *intended* to do it—that he has ever made up his mind to *obey* me ; he only means, "I have been willing to try—I made up my mind to try to be willing ;" that is all ! "O," he says, "I have brought myself to be willing to try to will to do it."

So you say—I have tried to get religion. And what *is* religion that you could not get it ? How did you fail ? You have been trying, probably, in this way. God has said, "Give me thy heart," and you turned round and asked God to do it Himself, or perhaps you simply waited for Him to do it. He commanded you to repent, and you have tried to get Him to repent for you. He said, Believe the Gospel, and you have only been thinking of getting Him to believe for you. No wonder you have tried for a long time in vain. How could it be otherwise ? You have not been trying to do what God commanded you to do, but to induce God to change His system of moral government and put Himself in your place to do Himself the duty He enjoins upon you. What a miserable perversion is this.

Now, as to this whole plea of having tried to be a Christian, what is the use of it? You will easily see its use when you realize duly:

(1.) That it is utterly false when understood as you intend it.

(2.) That it is a foul implication of the character of God.

You say—Lord, I know I can't—I have tried all I can, and I know I cannot become a Christian. I am willing to get religion, but I cannot make it out.

Who, then, is to blame? Not yourself, according to your statement of your case. Where, then, is the blame? Let me ask—what would be said in the distant regions of the universe if you were believed there, when you say, I have tried with all my heart to love and serve God, but I can't?

But they never can believe such a libel on their own infinite Father! Of course they will pronounce your doom as you deserve.

13. Another excuses himself by the plea—*it will do no good to try*. And what do you mean by this? Do you mean that God will not pay well for service done Him? Or do you mean that He will not forgive you if you do repent? Do you think (as some do) that you have sinned away your day of grace?

Well, suppose you have; is this any reason why you should go on in sin? Do you not believe that God is good? O, yes. And that He will forgive you if the good of the universe admits? Most certainly. Then is the impossibility of His forgiving you any reason why you should go on in sin for ever, and for ever rage against a God of infinite goodness? You believe Him to be compassionate and forgiving; then should you not say, I will at least stop sinning against *such a God!* Why not say with the man who dreamed that he was just going to hell, and as he was parting with his brother—going, as his dream had it, to heaven, he said—"I am going down to hell, but I want you to tell God from me that I am greatly obliged to Him for ten thousand mercies which I never deserved ; He has never done me the least injustice ; give Him my thanks for all the unmerited good He has done me." At this point he awoke, and found himself bathed in tears of repentance and gratitude to his Father in heaven. O, if men would only act as reasonably as that man dreamed, it would be noble—it would be *right*. If, when they suppose themselves to have sinned away the day of grace, they would say, " I know God is good—I will at least send Him my thanks—He has done me no injustice." If they would take this course they might have at least the satisfaction of feeling that it is a reasonable and a fit one in their circumstances. Sinner, will you do this?

14. Another, closely pressed, says, *" I have offered to give my heart to Christ, but He won't receive me. I have no evidence that He receives me or ever will."* In the last inquiry meeting, a young woman told me she had offered to give her heart to the Lord, but He would not receive her. This was charging the lie directly upon Christ, for He has said—" Him that cometh to Me, I will in no wise cast out." You say, I came and offered myself, and He would not receive me. Jesus Christ says, " Behold I stand at the door and knock ; if *any* man "—not if some particular, some favoured one—but if *any man* " hear my voice and open the door, I will come in to him." And yet when you offered Him your heart, did He spurn you away? Did He say—*Away*, sinner, BEGONE? No, sinner, He never did it, *never*. He has said He never would do it. His own words are, " Him that cometh unto Me, *I will in no wise cast out*." " He that seeketh, findeth : to him that knocketh it shall be opened." But you say, I have sought and I did not find. Do you mean to make

out that Jesus Christ is a liar ? Have you charged this upon Him to His very face ? Do you make your solemn affirmation—"Lord, I did seek—I laid myself at Thy gate and knocked—but all in vain ?" And do you mean to bring this excuse of yours as a solemn charge of falsehood against Jesus Christ and against God ? This will be a serious business with you before it is done with.

15. But another says—"*There is no salvation for me.*" Do you mean that Christ has made no atonement for you ? But he says, He tasted death for every man. It is declared that God so loved the world that He gave His only begotten Son that *whomsoever* believeth on Him shall have eternal life. And now do you affirm that there is no salvation provided and possible for you ? Are you mourning all your way down to hell because you cannot possibly have salvation ? When the cup of salvation is placed to your lips, do you dash it away, saying, That cannot be for me ? And do you *know* this ? Can you prove it even against the word of God Himself ? Stand forth, then, if there be such a sinner on this footstool of God—speak it out, if you have such a charge against God, and if you can prove it true. Ah, is there no hope ? none at all ? Oh, the difficulty is not that there is no salvation provided for and offered to you, but that there is no heart for it. "Wherefore is there a price put into the hands of a fool to get wisdom, seeing he hath no heart for it ?"

16. But perhaps you say in excuse—"*I cannot change my own heart.*" Cannot ? Suppose Adam had made this excuse when God called him to repent after his first sin. "Make you a new heart and a right spirit," said the Lord to him. "I cannot change my own heart myself," replies Adam. Indeed, responds his Maker, how long is it since you changed your heart yourself ? You changed it a few hours ago from holiness to sin, and will you tell your Creator that you can't change it from sin to holiness ?

The sinner should consider that the change of heart is a voluntary thing. You must do it for yourself or it is never done. True, there is a sense in which God changes the heart, but it is only this : God influences the sinner to change, and then the sinner does it. The change is the sinner's own voluntary act.

17. You say, again, *you can't change your heart without more conviction.* Do you mean by this that you have not knowledge enough of your duty and your sin ? You cannot say this. You do know your sin and your duty. You know you ought to consecrate yourself to God. What, then, do you mean ? Can't you do that which you know you ought to do ? Ah, there is the old lie—that shameless refuge of lies—that same foul dogma of *inability.* What is implied in this new form of it ? This—that God is not willing to convict you enough to make it possible for you to repent. There is a work and a responsibility for God, and He will not do His work—will not bear His responsibility. Hence, you, alas, have no alternative but to go down to hell. All because God will not do His part towards your salvation ! *Do you really believe that, sinner ?*

18. Again, you say in excuse, *that you must first have more of the Spirit.* And yet you resist the Spirit every day. God offers you His Spirit, nay, more, God *bestows* His Spirit ; but you resist it. What, then, do you mean when you pretend to want more of the Spirit's influence ?

The truth is, you do not want it—you only want to make it appear that God does not do His part to help you to repent, and that as you can't repent without His help, therefore the blame of your impenitence rests on God. It is only another refuge of lies—another form of the old slander upon God—He has made me unable and won't help me out of my inability.

19. The sinner also excuses himself by saying—*God must change my heart.* But in the sense in which God requires

you to do it, He cannot do it Himself. God is said to change the heart only in the sense of persuading you to do it. As in a man's change of politics, one might say—"Such a man changed my heart—he brought me over," which, how-ever, by no means implies that you did not change your own mind. The plain meaning is that he persuaded, and you yielded.

But this plea made by the sinner as his excuse implies that there is something more for God to do before the sinner can become religious. I have heard many professors of religion take this very ground. Yes, thousands of Christian ministers, too, have said to the sinner—"Wait for God ; He will change your heart in His own good time ; you can't do it yourself, and all that you can do is to put yourself in the way for the Lord to change your heart. When this time comes, He will give you a new heart, while you are asleep, perhaps, in a state of unconsciousness. God acts in this matter as a sovereign, and does His own work in His own way."

So they teach—filling the mouth of the sinner with excuses and making his heart like an adamant against the real claims of God upon his conscience.

20. The sinner pleads, again "*I can't live a Christian life if I were to become a Christian. It is unreasonable for me to expect to succeed where I see so many fail.*" I recollect the case of a man who said, "It is of no use for me to repent and be a Christian, for it is altogether irrational for me to expect to do better than others have done before me." So sinners who make this excuse come forward very modestly and tell God—"I am very humble ; Thou seest, Lord, that I have a very low opinion of myself ; I am so zealous of Thine honour, and so afraid that I shall bring disgrace upon Thy cause ; it does not seem at all best for me to think of be-coming a Christian, I have such a horror of dishonouring Thy name.

Yes ; and what then ? "Therefore, I will sin on and trample the blessed Gospel under my feet. I will persecute Thee, O my God, and make war on Thy cause, for it is better by far not to profess religion than to profess and then disgrace my profession." What logic ! Fair specimen of the absurdity of the sinner's excuses.

This excuse assumes that there is not grace enough provided and offered to sustain the soul in a Christian life. The doctrine is, that it is irrational to expect that we can, by any grace received in this life, perfectly obey the law of God. There is not grace and help enough afforded by God ! And this is taught as BIBLE THEOLOGY ! Away with such teaching to the nether pit whence it came !

What ! is God so weak that He can't hold up the soul that casts itself on Him ? Or is He so parsimonious in bestowing His gracious aid that it must be expected always to fall short of meeting the wants of His dependent and depending child ? So you seem to suppose. So hard to persuade the Lord to give you a particle of grace ! Can't get grace enough to live a Christian life with honour ! What is this but charging God of withholding sufficient grace.

But what say the word and the oath of Jehovah ? We read that "God, willing more abundantly to show unto the heirs of promise the immutability of His counsel, confirmed it by an oath ; that by two immutable things in which it is impossible for God to lie, we might have strong consolation who have fled for refuge to lay hold upon the hope set before us." You say, however, "If I should flee and lay hold of this hope I should fail for want of grace. I could have no 'consolation' in reposing upon the word of Him who cannot lie. The oath of the immutable God can never suffice for me."

So you belie the word of God, and make up a miserably lim and guilty apology for your impenitence.

21. Another excuse claims that *this is a very dark, myste-*

rious subject. This matter of faith and regeneration—I can't understand it.

Sinner, did you ever meet the Lord with this objection, and say, "Lord, Thou hast required me to do things which I can't understand?" You know that you can understand well enough that you are a sinner—that Christ died for you —that you must believe on Him and break off your sins by repentance. All this is so plain that "the wayfaring man, though a fool, need not err therein." Your plea, therefore, is as false as it is foul. It is nothing better than a base libel on God!

22. But you say, "*I can't believe.*" You mean (do you?) that you can't believe a God of infinite veracity as you can believe a fellow man? Would you imply that God asks you to believe things that are really incredible—things so revolting to reason that you cannot admit them on any testimony that even God himself can adduce?

And do you expect to make out this case against God? Do you even believe the first point in it yourself?

But you urge again that you can't *realize these things.* You know these things to be true, but you can't realize— you can't realize that the Bible is true—that God does offer to forgive—that salvation is actually provided and placed within your reach. What help can there be for a case like yours? What can make these truths more certain? But, on your own showing, you do not want more evidence. Why not, then, act upon the known truth? What more can you ask?

Do you ever carry your case before God and say, "O Lord, Thou sayest that Christ died for me, but I can't realize that it is so; and, therefore, Lord, I can't possibly embrace Him as my Saviour?" Would this be a rational excuse?

But you also plead that *you can't repent.* You can't be sorry you have abused God. You can't make up your mind now to break off from all sin. If this be really so, then you cannot make up your mind to obey God, and you may as well make up your mind to *go to hell !* There is no alternative !

But at any rate, you can't become a Christian *now.* You mean to be converted some time, but you can't make up your mind to it NOW. Well, God requires it now, and of course you must yield or abide the consequences.

But do you say, You can't now ? Then God is very much to blame for asking it. If, however, the truth be that you can, then the lie is on your side, and it is a most infamous and abusive lie against your Maker.

III. All excuses for sin add insult to injury.

1. A plea that reflects injuriously upon the court or the lawgiver is an aggravation of the original crime. It is always so regarded in all tribunals. It must be pre-eminently so between the sinner and his infinite Lawgiver and Judge.

2. The same is true of any plea made in self-justification. If it be false, it is considered an aggravation of the crime charged. This is a case which sometimes happens, and whenever it does, it is deemed to add fresh insult and wrong. For a criminal to come and spread out his lie upon the records of the court—to declare what he knows to be false ; nothing can prejudice his case so fearfully.

On the other hand, when a man before the court appears to be honest, and confesses his guilt, the judge, if he has any discretion in the case, puts down his sentence to the lowest point possible. But if the criminal resorts to dodging—if he equivocates and lies, then you will see the strong arm of the law come down upon him. The judge comes forth in all the thunders of judicial majesty and terror, and feels that he *may* not spare his victim. Why ? The man has lied before the very court of justice. The man sets himself against all law, and he must be put down, or law itself is down.

3. It is truly abominable for the sinner to abuse God, and then excuse himself for it. Ah, this is only the old way of the guilty. Adam and Eve in the garden fled and hid themselves when they heard the voice of the Lord approaching. And what had they done? The Lord calls them out and begins to search them : " Adam, what hast thou done? Has thou eaten of the forbidden tree in the centre of the garden?" Adam quailed, but fled to an excuse : '" The woman whom *Thou gavest to be with me,* she gave me of the tree and I did eat." God, he says, gave him his tempter. God, according to his excuse, had been chiefly to blame in the transaction.

Next He turns to the woman : " What is that thou hast done?" She, too, has an excuse : " The serpent beguiled me and I did eat." Ah, this perpetual shuffling the blame back upon God ! It has been kept up through the long line of Adam's imitators down to this day. For six thousand years God has been hearing it, and still the world is spared, and the vengeance of God has not yet burst forth to smite all His guilty calumniators to hell ! O ! what patience in God ! And who have ever abused His patience and insulted Him by their excuses more than sinners in this house ?

CONCLUSION

1. No sinner under the light of the Gospel lives a single hour in sin without some excuse, either tacit or avowed, by which he justifies himself. It seems to be a law of man's intelligent nature that when accused of wrong, either by his conscience or by any other agent, he must either confess or justify. The latter is the course taken by all impenitent sinners. Hence, the reason why they have so much occasion for excuses, and why they find it convenient to have so great a variety. It is remarkable with what facility they fly from one to another, as if these refuges of lies might make up in

number what they lack in strength.   Conscious that not one
of all the multitude is valid in point of truth and right, they
yet, when pressed on one, fly to another, and when driven from
all in succession they are ready to come back and fight the
same ground over again.   It is so hard to abandon all excuses
and admit the humbling truth that they themselves are all
wrong and God all right.

Hence, it becomes the great business of a Gospel minister
to search out and expose the sinner's excuses; to go all round
and round, and, if possible, demolish the sinner's refuges of
lies, and lay his heart open to the shafts of truth.

2. *Excuses render repentance impossible.*   For excuses are
justifications; and who does not know that justification is the
very opposite of confession and repentance?   To seek after
and embrace excuses, therefore, is to place one's self at the
farthest possible remove from repentance.

Of course the self-accusing sinner makes it impossible for
God to forgive him.   He places the Deity in such a position
toward himself, and, I might say, places himself in such an
attitude toward the government of God, that his forgiveness
would be ruin to the very throne of God.   What would
heaven say, and hell too, and earth besides, if God were to
forgive a sinner while he, by his excuses, is justifying himself
and condemning his Maker?

3. *Sinners should lay all their excuses at once before God.*
Surely this is most reasonable.   Why not?   If a man owed
me, and supposed he had a reasonable excuse for not paying
the debt, he should come to me and let me understand the
whole case.   Perhaps he will satisfy me that his views are
right.

Now, sinner, have you ever done so in regard to God?
Have you ever brought up one excuse before the Lord, saying,
" Thou requirest me to be holy, but I can't be ; Lord, I have
a good excuse for not obeying Thee ?"   No, sinner; you are
not in the habit of doing this—probably you have not done it

the first time yet in all your life. In fact, you have no particular encouragement to carry your excuses before God, for you have not one yet that you yourself believe to be good for anything except to answer the purpose of a refuge of lies. Your excuses won't stand the ordeal of your own reason and conscience. How then can you hope they will stand before the searching eye of Jehovah? The fact that you never come with your excuses to God shows that you have no confidence in them.

4. *What infinite madness to rest on excuses which you dare not bring before God now!* How can you stand before God in the judgment, if your excuses are so mean that you cannot seriously think of bringing one of them before God in this world? O, sinner, that coming day will be far more searching and awful than anything you have seen yet. See that dense mass of sinners drawn up before the great white throne—far as the eye can sweep they come surging up—a countless throng; and now they stand, and the awful trump of God summons them forward to bring forth their excuses for sin. Ho, sinners—any one of you, all—what have you to say why sentence should not be passed on you? Where are all those excuses you were once so free and bold to make? Where are they all? Why don't you make them now? *Hark!* God waits; He listens; there is silence in heaven—all through the congregated throng—for half an hour—an awful silence—that may be felt; but not a word—not a moving lip among the gathered myriads of sinners there; and now the great and dreadful Judge arises and lets loose His thunders. O, see the waves of dire damnation roll over the ocean-masses of self-condemned sinners! Did you ever see the judge rise from his bench in court to pass sentence of death on a criminal? There, see, the poor man reels—he falls prostrate—there is no longer any strength in him, for death is on him and his last hope has perished!

O, sinner, when that sentence from the dread throne shall

fall on thee! Your excuses are as millstones around your neck as you plunge along down the sides of the pit to the nethermost hell!

5. *Sinners don't need their excuses.* God does not ask for even one. He does not require you to justify yourself— not at all. If you needed them for your salvation I could sympathize with you, and certainly would help you all I could. But you don't need them. Your salvation does not turn on your successful self-vindication. You need not rack your brain for excuses. Better say, I don't want them— don't deserve them—have not one that is worth a straw. Better say, " *I am wicked.* God knows that's the truth, and it were vain for me to attempt to conceal it. I AM WICKED, and if I ever live, it must be on simple mercy !"

I can recollect very well the year I lived on excuses, and how long it was before I gave them up. I had never heard a minister preach on the subject. I found, however, by my experience, that my excuses and lies were the obstacles in the way of my conversion. As soon as I let these go utterly, I found the gate of mercy wide open. And so, sinner, would you.

6. *Sinners ought to be ashamed of their excuses, and repent of them.* Perhaps you have not always seen this as plainly as you may now. With the light now before you it becomes you to beware. See to it that you never make another excuse, unless you intend to abuse God in the most horrible manner. Nothing can be a more grievous abomination in the sight of God than excuses made by a sinner who knows they are utterly false and blasphemous. O, you ought to repent of the insult you have already offered to God—and NOW, too, lest you find yourself thrust away from the gate of mercy.

7. *You admit your obligation, and of course are estopped from making excuses.* For if you have any good excuse, you are not under obligation. If any one of you has a good

excuse for disobeying God, you are no longer under obligation to obey. But since you are compelled to admit obligation, you are also compelled to relinquish excuses.

8. Inasmuch as you do and must admit your obligation, then if you still plead excuses you insult God to His face. You insult Him by charging Him with infinite tyranny.

Now, what use do you calculate to make of this sermon? Are you ready to say, "I will henceforth desist from all my excuses, now and for ever ; and God shall have my whole heart ? What do you say ? Will you set about to hunt up some new excuse ? Do you at least say, "Let me go home first—don't press me to yield to God here on the spot—let me go home and then I will?" Do you say this ? And are you aware how tender is this moment—how critical this passing hour ? Remember it is not I who press this claim upon you—but it is God. God Himself commands you to repent to-day—*this hour*. You know your duty—you know what religion is—what it is to give God your heart. And now I come to the final question : *Will you do it ?* Will you abandon all your excuses, and fall, a self-condemned sinner, before a God of love, and yield to him yourself—your heart, and your whole being, henceforth and for ever ? WILL YOU COME ?

4

THE SINNER'S
EXCUSES ANSWERED

"Elihu also proceeded and said, Suffer me a little, and I will shew thee that I have yet to speak on God's behalf. I will fetch my knowledge from afar, and will ascribe righteousness to my Maker."—*Job* xxxvi. 1—*3*

ELIHU was present and heard the controversy between Job and his friends. The latter maintained that God's dealings with Job proved him wicked. This Job denied, and maintained that we could not judge men to be good or bad, from God's providential dealings with them, because facts show that the present is not a state of rewards and punishments. They, however, regarded this as taking part with the wicked, and hence did not shrink from accusing Job of doing this.

Elihu had previously said—My desire is that Job may be tried in regard to what he has said of wicked men. But ere the discussion closed, he saw that Job had confounded his three friends, maintaining unanswerably that it was not because of any hypocrisy or special guilt that he was so signally scourged. Yet plainly even Job had not the key to explain the reason of God's dealings with him. To him it was still a mystery. He did not see that God might have been seeking to test and discipline his piety, or even to make an example of his integrity and submissiveness to confound the devil with.

Elihu purposed to speak in God's behalf and ascribed righteousness to his Maker. It is my present object to do the same in regard to sinners who refuse to repent, and who

complain of God's ways. But before I proceed, let me advert
to a fact. Some years since, in my labours as an evangelist,
I became acquainted with a man prominent in the place of
his residence for his general intelligence, and whose two
successive wives were daughters of Old School Presbyterian
clergymen. Through them he had received many books to read
on religious subjects, which they and their friends supposed
would do him good, but which failed to do him any good at
all. He denied the inspiration of the Bible, and on grounds
which those books did not in his view obviate at all. Indeed,
they only served to aggravate his objections.

When I came into the place, his wife was very anxious that
I should see and converse with him. I called ; she sent for
him to come in and see the new minister ; to which he
replied that he was sure he could do him no good, since he had
conversed with so many and found no light on the points
that so much stumbled him ; but upon her urgent entreaty, he
consented for her sake to come in. I said to him in the
outset, " Don't understand me as having called here to have
a quarrel with you, and provoke a dispute. I only wish at your
wife's request to converse with you, if you are perfectly
willing, upon the great subject of divine revelation." He
signified his pleasure to have such a conversation, and
accordingly I asked him to state briefly his position. He
replied—" I admit the truths of natural religion, and believe
most fully in the immortality of the soul, but not in the inspiration of the Scriptures. I am a Deist." But, said I, on what
ground do you deny the inspiration of the Bible ? Said he, I
know it cannot be true. *How* do you know that ? It contradicts
the affirmations of my reason. You admit and I hold that God
created my nature, both physical and moral. Here is a book,
said to be from God, but it contradicts my nature. I therefore know it cannot be from God.

This of course opened the door for me to draw from him
the particular points of his objection to the Bible as teaching

what his nature contradicted. These points and my reply to them will constitute the body of my present discourse.

1. The Bible cannot be true because it *represents God as unjust.* I find myself possessed of convictions as to what is just and unjust. These convictions the Bible outrages. It represents God as creating men and then condemning them for another's sin.

Indeed, said I, and where? Say, where does the Bible affirm this?

Why, does it not? said he. No. Are you a Presbyterian? said he? Yes. He then began to quote the catechism. Stop, stop, said I, that is not the Bible. That is only a human catechism. True, said he, but does not the Bible connect the universal sin of the race with the sin of Adam? Yes, said I, it does in a particular way, but it is quite essential to our purpose to understand in *what way.* The Bible makes this connection *incidental* and not direct; and it always represents the sinner condemned as really sinning himself, and as condemned *for his own sin.*

But, continued he, children do suffer for their father's sins. Yes, said I, in a certain sense it is so, and must'be so. Do you not see yourself, everywhere, that children must suffer for the sins of their parents? and be blessed also by the piety of their parents? You see this and you find no fault with it. You see that children must be implicated in the good or ill conduct of their parents; their relation as children makes this absolutely unavoidable. Is it not wise and good that the happiness or misery of children should depend on their parents, and thus become one of the strongest possible motives to them to train them up in virtue? Yet it is true that the son is never rewarded or punished *punitively* for his parents' sins. The evil that befalls him through his connection with his parents is always disciplinary—never punitive.

Again, he said, the Bible certainly represents God as creating men sinners, and as condemning them for their sinful nature. No, replied I; for the Bible defines sin as voluntary transgression of law, and it is absurd to suppose that a *nature* can be a voluntary transgressor.   Besides, it is in the nature of the case impossible that God *should make a sinful nature*. It is in fact doubly impossible, for the thing is a natural impossibility, and if it were not, it would yet be *morally* impossible that he should do it.   He could not do it for the same reason that He can not sin.

In harmony with this is the fact that the Bible never represents God as condemning men for their nature, either here or at the judgment.   Nowhere in the Bible is there the least intimation that God holds men responsible for their created nature, but only for the vile and pertinacious abuse of their nature.   Other views of this matter, differing from this, are not the Bible, but are only false glosses put upon it usually by those whose philosophy has led them into absurd interpretations.   Everywhere in the Bible men are condemned only for their voluntary sins, and are required to repent of these sins, and of these only.   Indeed, there can possibly be no other sins than these.

Again, it is said, the Bible represents God as being *cruel*, inasmuch as He commanded the Jews to wage a war of extermination against the ancient Canaanites.

But why should this be called cruel?   The Bible expressly informs us that God commanded this because of their awful wickedness.   They were too awfully wicked to live.   God could not suffer them to defile the earth and corrupt society. Hence He arose in His zeal for human welfare, and commanded to wash the land clean of such unutterable abominations.   The good of the race demanded it.   Was this cruel?   Nay, verily, this was simply benevolent.   It was one of the highest acts of benevolence to smite down such a race and sweep them from the face of the earth.   And to employ the Jews as His executioners, giving them to understand distinctly *why* He commanded them to do it, was putting them in a way to derive the highest moral benefit from the transaction. In no other way could they have been so solemnly impressed with the holy justice of Jehovah. And now will any man find fault with God for this? None can do so, *reasonably.*

But the Bible allows slavery.

What? The Bible allow slavery? In what sense allow it? and under what circumstances? and what kind of slavery? These are all very important inquiries if we wish to know the certainty and the meaning of the things we say.

The Bible did indeed allow the Jews, in the case of captives taken in war, to commute death for servitude. When the customs of existing nations put captives taken in war to death, God authorized the Jews in certain cases to spare their captives and employ them as servants. By this means they were taken out from among idolatrous nations and brought into contact with the worship and ordinances of the true God.

Moreover, God enacted statutes for the protection of the Hebrew servant, which made his case infinitely better than being cut off in his sins. And who shall call this cruel? Jewish servitude was not American slavery, nor scarcely an approximation toward it. It would require too much time to go into the detail of this subject here. All that I have stated might be abundantly substantiated.

Again, it is objected God is unmerciful, vindictive, and implacable. The gentleman to whom I have alluded said—I don't believe the Bible is from God when it represents Him as so vindictive and implacable that He would not forgive sin until He had first taken measures to kill His own Son.

Now it was by no means unnatural that, under such instructions he had received, he should think so. I had felt so myself. This very objection had· stumbled me. But I afterwards saw the answer so plainly that it left nothing more to be desired. The answer indeed is exceedingly plain. It was not an implacable disposition in God which led Him to require the death of Christ as the ground of forgiveness.   It was simply his benevolent regard for the safety and blessedness of His kingdom. He knew very well that it was unsafe to forgive sin without such a satisfaction. Indeed, this was the strongest possible exhibition of a forgiving disposition, to consent to the sacrifice of His Son for this purpose. He loved His Son, and certainly would not inflict one needless pang upon Him. He also loved a sinning race, and saw the depth of that ruin toward which they were rushing. Therefore He longed to forgive them, and to prepare a way in which He could do so with safety. He only desired to avoid all misapprehension. To forgive without such atonement as would adequately express His abhorrence of sin, would leave the intelligent universe to think that He did not care how much any beings should sin. This would not do.

Let it be considered also that the giving up of Jesus Christ was only a voluntary offering on God's part to sustain law, so that He could forgive without peril to His government. Jesus was not in any sense *punished ;* He only *volunteered* to suffer for sinners that they might be freed from the governmental necessity of suffering. And was not mercy manifested in this ?   Certainly.   How could it be manifested more signally ?

But, says the objector, God is unjust, inasmuch as He requires impossibilities on pain of endless death.

Does He, indeed ? Then *where ?* In the law, is it, or in the Gospel ? In these taken together we have the aggregate of all God's requirements. In what part, then, of either law or Gospel do you find the precept contained which requires impossibilities ? Is it in the law ? But the law says only— "Thou shall love the Lord thy God *with all thy heart ;*" not with another man's heart, but simply with thine own ; only with *all* thine own heart, not with more than all. Read on still further : " and with all thy strength." Not with the strength of an angel—not with the strength of any other being than thyself, and only with such an amount of strength as you actually have for the time being. The demands of the law, you see, exactly meet your ability; nothing more and nothing else.

Indeed, said he, this is a new view of the subject. Well; but is not this just as it should be? Does not the law carry with it its own vindication in its very terms? How can any one say that the law requires of us impossible service—things we have no power to do? The fact is, it requires us to do just what we can and nothing more. Where, then, is this objection to the Bible? Where is the impossibility of which you speak?

But, resumed he, is it not true that "no mere man since the fall has been able wholly to keep the commandments of God, but doth daily break them in thought, word, and deed?"

Ah, my friend, that's catechism, not Bible; we must be careful not to impute to the Bible all that human catechisms have said. The Bible only requires you to consecrate to God what strength and powers you actually have, and is by no means responsible for the affirmation that God requires of man more than he can do. No, verily, the Bible nowhere imputes to God a requisition so unreasonable and cruel. No wonder the human mind should rebel against such a view of God's law. If any human law were to require impossibilities, there could be no end to the denunciations that must fall upon it. No human mind could possibly approve of such a law. Nor can it be supposed that God can reasonably act on principles which would disgrace and ruin any human government.

But, resumed he, here is another objection. The Bible represents men as unable to believe the Gospel unless they are drawn by God, for it reads—"No man can come to me except the Father who hath sent me draw him." Yet sinners are required to believe on pain of damnation. How is this?

To this the reply is, first, the connection shows that Christ

referred to drawing by means of teaching or instruction ; for
to confirm what He had said, He appeals to the ancient
scriptures—" It is written, They shall all be taught of God."
Without this teaching, then, none can come. They must
know Christ before they can come to Him in faith. They
cannot believe till they know what to believe. In this sense
of coming, untaught heathen are not required to come. God
never requires any to come, who have not been taught. Once
taught, they are bound to come, may be and are required to
come, and are without excuse if they refuse.

But, replied he, the Bible does really teach that men
cannot serve the Lord, and still it holds them responsible
for doing it. Joshua said to all the people, " Ye cannot
serve the Lord, for He is an holy God."

Let us see. Joshua had called all the people together and
had laid before them their obligation to serve the Lord
their God. When they all said so readily and with so little
serious consideration that they would, Joshua replied—" Ye
cannot serve the Lord for He is a holy God ; He is a jealous
God ; He will not forgive your transgressions nor your sins."
What did he mean ? Plainly this—Ye cannot serve God,
because you have not heartily abandoned your sins. You
cannot get along with a God so holy and so jealous, unless you
give up sinning. You cannot serve God with a selfish heart.
You cannot please Him till you really renounce your sins
altogether. You must begin by making to yourselves a new
heart. Joshua doubtless saw that they had not given up
their sins and had not really begun to serve God at all, and
did not even understand the first principles of true religion.
This is the reason why he seemed to repulse them so suddenly.
It is as if he would say—Stop ; you must go back and begin
with utterly putting away all your sins. You cannot serve
a holy and jealous God in any other way, for He will not
go along with you as His people if you persist in sinning
against Him.

It is a gross perversion of the Bible to make it mean that men have no power to do what God requires. It is true indeed, that in this connection it sometimes uses the words *can* and *can not*, but these and similar words should be construed according to the nature of the subject. All reasonable men construe thus intuitively in all common use of language. The Bible always employs the language of common life and in the way of common usage. Hence it should be thus interpreted.

When it is said that Joseph's brethren hated him and *could not* speak peaceably to him, the meaning is not that their organs of speech could not articulate kind words ; but it points us to a difficulty *in the heart.* They *hated* him so badly they could not speak pleasantly. Nor does the sacred historian assume that they could not at once subdue this hatred and treat Joseph as brother should treat brother. The sacred writers are the last men in the world to apologize for sin on this wise.

There is the case of the angels sent to hasten Lot out of guilty Sodom. One said, " Haste thee, escape thither, for I can not do anything until thou be come thither." Does this mean that the Almighty God had no *power* to overwhelm Sodom so long as Lot was in it ? Certainly not. It meant only that it was His purpose not to destroy the city till Lot was out. Indeed, all men use language thus in common life. You go into one of our village stores and say to the merchant, Can you lift a ton of your goods at once ? No. Can you sell me that piece of cloth for a shilling a yard ? No. Does this " *can* " mean the same as the other ? By no means. But how is it that you detect the difference ? How is it that you come to know so readily which is the physical *cannot* and which the *moral ?* The nature of the subject tells you.

But, you say, the same word ought always to mean the same thing. Well, if it ought to, it does not, in any language ever yet spoken by man. And yet there is no difficulty in understanding even the most imperfect of human languages if men are honest in speaking and honest in hearing, and will use their common sense. They intuitively construe language according to the nature of the subject spoken of.

The Bible always assumes that sinners can not do right and please God *with a wicked heart.* It always takes the ground that God abhors hypocrisy—that He can not be satisfied with mere forms and professions of service when the *heart* is not in it, and hence that all acceptable service must begin with making a new and sincere heart.

But here is another difficulty. Can I make to myself a new heart?

Yes, and you could not doubt but that you could, if you only understood what the language means and what the thing is.

See Adam and Eve in the garden. What was their *heart?* Did God create it? No; it is not possible that He should, for a heart in this sense is not the subject of physical creation. When God made Adam, giving him all the capacities for acting morally, he had no heart good or bad until he came to act morally. When did he first have a moral heart? When he first waked to moral consciousness and gave his heart to God. When first he saw God manifested, and put confidence in Him as his Father, and yielded up his heart to Him in love and obedience. Observe, he first had this holy heart because he yielded up his will to God in entire consecration. This was his first holy heart.

But at length the hour of temptation came, alluring him to withdraw his heart from God and turn to pleasing himself. To Eve the tempter said—" Hath God indeed said—Ye shall not surely die?" Ah, is that so? Then he raised the question either as to the fact that God had really threatened death for sin, or as to the *justice* of doing so. In either case it raised a question about obedience and opened the heart to temptation. Then that fruit came before her mind. It was fair and seemed good for food. Her appetite enkindles and clamours for indulgence. Then, it was said to be fitted to "make one wise," and by eating it she might "be as the gods, knowing good and evil." This appealed to her curiosity. Yielding to this temptation and making up her mind to please herself, she made herself a new heart of *sin ;* she changed her heart from holiness to sin, and fell from her first moral position. When Adam yielded to temptation, he made the same change in his heart ; he gave himself up to selfishness and sin. This accounts for all future acts of selfishness in after life.

Adam and Eve are again brought before God. God says to Adam—Give me thy heart. Change your heart. What ! says Adam, I cannot change my own heart ! But God replies, How long is it since you have done it ? It is but yesterday that you changed your own heart from holiness to sin ; why can't you change it back ?

So in all cases. Changing the ruling preference, the governing purpose of the mind, is the thing, and who can say, I cannot do that. Cannot you do that ? Cannot you give yourself to God ?

The reason you cannot please God in your executive acts, is that your governing purpose is not right. While your leading motive is wrong, all you do is selfish, because it is all done for the single object of pleasing yourself. You do nothing for the sake of pleasing God, and with the governing design and purpose of doing all His holy will ; hence all you do, even your religious duties, only displease God. If the Bible had anywhere represented God as being pleased with your hypocritical services it would be proven false, for this is perfectly impossible.

But you say, the Bible requires me to begin with the inner man—the heart—and you say you cannot get at this ; that you cannot reach your own heart or will to change it.

Indeed, you are entirely mistaken. This is the very thing

that is most entirely within your power. Of all things conceivable, this is the very thing that you can do most certainly—that is most absolutely within your power. If God had made your salvation turn upon your walking across the room, you might not be able to do it; or if upon lifting your eyelids or rising from your seat, or any the least movement of your muscles, you might be utterly unable to do it. You could *will* the motion required, and you could try; but the muscles might have no power to act. You often think that if God had only conditioned your salvation upon some motions of your muscles, it would have been so easy; if He had only asked you to control the *outside;* but, oh, you say, how can I control the *inside?* The inside is the very thing you can move and control. If it had been the outside, you might strive and groan till you die, and not be able to move a muscle, even on pain of an eternal hell. But now inasmuch as God only says, " *Change your will,*" all is brought within your control. This is just the thing you always *can* do; you can always move your will. You can always give your heart, at your own option. Where, then, is your difficulty and objection? God requires you to act with your freedom; to exercise the powers of free voluntary action that He has given you. He asks you to put your hand on the fountain-head of all your own power, to act just where your central power lies—where you ALWAYS HAVE POWER so long as you have a rational mind and a moral nature. Your liberty does not consist in a power to move your muscles at pleasure, for the connection between your muscles and your will may be broken, and at all events is always necessary when your body is in its normal state; therefore God does not require you to perform any particular movement of the muscles, but only to *change your will.* This, compared with all other things, is that which you can always do, and can do more surely than anything else.

Again, considering volitions as distinct from ultimate purposes, and as standing next before executive acts, it is not volitions that God requires, but He lays His requisition directly upon the *ultimate purposes*. The ultimate purposes being given, these subordinate volitions follow naturally and necessarily. Your liberty, therefore, does not, strictly speaking, lie in these subordinate volitions—such as the volition to sit, to walk, to speak. But the ultimate purpose controlling all volition, and relating to the main object you shall pursue, as, for example, whether you shall in all things strive to please God, or, on the other hand, strive to please yourself; this being the precise point wherein your liberty of free action lies, is the very point upon which God lays his moral requisitions. The whole question is, will you please God, or please yourself? Will you give your heart to Him, or give it to your own selfish enjoyment?

So long as you give your heart to selfish pleasure and withhold it from God, it will be perfectly natural for you to sin. This is precisely the reason why it is so natural for sinners to sin. It is because the will, the heart, is set upon it, and all they have to do is to carry out this ruling propensity and purpose. But, just change this governing purpose, and you will find obedience equally natural and equally easy in all its executive acts. It will then become natural to please God in everything. *Now* pleasing yourself is natural enough. Why? Because you are consecrated to pleasing yourself. But change this purpose; make a new and totally opposite consecration; reverse the committed *heart*, and let it be for God and not for self; then all duty will be easy for the same reason that all sin is so easy now.

So far is it from being true that you are unable to make your heart new, the fact is you would long ago have done it if you had not resisted God in His efforts to move you to repentance. Do you not know that you have often resisted God's Spirit? You know it well. So clear were your convictions that you *ought* to live for God, you had to resist every appeal of your own conscience, and march right in the face of known duty, and press your way along directly against God. If you had only listened to the voice of your reason, and to the demands of your conscience, you would have had a new heart long ago. But you resisted God when He tried to persuade you to have a new heart. O, sinner, how strong you have been to resist God ! How strong to resist every consideration addressed to your intelligence and to your reason! How strangely have you listened to the considerations for sinning ! O, the miserable petty things—tell me, what were they ? Suppose Christ should question you, and ask—What is there in earth that you should love it so well ? What in sin that you should prize it above my favour and my love ? What are those little indulgences—those very small things that always perish with the using ? Vanity of vanities, all is vanity. Most utterly contemptible ! You have been holding on to sin with no reasonable motive for so doing. But O, consider what motives you have fought against and resisted—motives of almost infinite force ! Think of the motives resulting from God's law—so excellent in itself, but so dreadful in its penalties against transgressors ; and then think also of God's infinite love in the Gospel ; how he opened the life-tides of His great heart, and let blessings flow with fulness like a God ! Yet consider how, despite of this love, you have abused your God exceedingly. You have gone on as if the motives to sin were all-persuasive, and as if sin's promises of good were more reliable than God's. When God spread out before you the glories of heaven, made all attractive and delightful in the beauties of holiness, you coolly replied— Earth is far better ! Give me earth while I can have it, and heaven only when I can have earth no longer ! O, sinner, you would have been converted a long time ago if you had not opposed God and trodden under foot His invitations and His appeals.

O, what a thing is this moral agency ! How awful its

power, and how momentous, therefore, must be its responsibilities. When God is pouring forth influences in waves of light and power, with a kind of moral omnipotence, you resist and withstand all ! As if you could do anything you pleased despite of God ! As if His influence were almost utterly powerless to move your heart from its fixed purpose to sin !

Does it require great strength to lay down your weapons? Indeed, this is quite a new thing ; for one would suppose it must rather require great strength to resist and to fight. And so you put forth your great strength in fighting against God, and would fain believe that you have not got strength enough to lay your weapons down ! O, the absurdity of sin and of the sinner's apology for sinning !

But you say—I must have the Holy Ghost. I answer, Yes ; but only to overcome your voluntary opposition. That is all.

After I had gone over this ground with my friend, as I have already explained, he became very much agitated. The sweat started from every pore ; his feelings overcame him ; he dropped his head down upon his knees, buried in intensest thought and full of emotion. I rose and went to the meeting. After it had progressed awhile he came in ; but O, how changed ! Said he, " Dear wife, I don't know what has become of my infidelity. I ought to be sent to hell ! What charges I have been making against God ! And yet with what amazing mercy did my God bear with me and let me live !" In fact, he found he had been all wrong and he broke all down and became as a little child before God.

And you, too, sinner, know you ought to live for God, yet you *have* not; you know that Jesus made Himself an offering to the injured dignity of that law which you violated, yet you have rejected Him. He gave Himself a voluntary offering, not to suffer the penalty of the law, but as your legal substitute ; and shall He have done all this in vain ? Do you say—" O, I'm so prejudiced against God and the Bible !" What, so prejudiced that you will not repent ? How horrible ! O let it suffice that you have played the fool so long and erred so exceedingly. It has been all wrong ! At once return and devote yourself to God. Why should you live to yourself at all ? You can get no good *so !*

Come to God—He is so easily pleased ! It is so much easier to please Him than to please and satisfy yourself. The veriest little child can please Him. Children often have the most delightful piety, because it is so simple-hearted. They know what to do to please God, and, meaning honestly to please Him, they can not fail. No matter how simple-hearted they are, if they mean to please God, they surely will.

And can not you at least do so much as honestly to choose and aim to please God ?

5

CONDITIONS OF BEING SAVED

"What must I do to be saved?"—*Acts* xvi. 30.

I BRING forward this subject to-day not because it is new to many in this congregation, but because it is greatly needed. I am happy to know that the great inquiry of our text is beginning to be deeply and extensively agitated in this community, and under these circumstances it is the first duty of a Christian pastor to answer it, fully and plainly.

The circumstances which gave occasion to the words of the text were briefly these. Paul and Silas had gone to Phillippi to preach the Gospel. Their preaching excited great opposition and tumult; they were arrested and thrown into prison, and the jailor was charged to keep them safely. At midnight they were praying and singing praises—God came down—the earth quaked and the prison rocked—its doors burst open, and their chains fell off; the jailor sprang up affrighted, and, supposing his prisoners had fled, was about to take his own life, when Paul cried out, "Do thyself no harm; we are all here." He then called for a light, and sprang in and came trembling, and fell down before Paul and Silas, and brought them out and said, "Sirs, what must I do to be saved?"

This is briefly the history of our text; and I improve it now, by showing,—

I. *What sinners must not do to be saved;* and

II. *What they must do.*

It has now come to be necessary and very important to tell men what they must *not* do in order to be saved. When the Gospel was first preached, Satan had not introduced as many delusions to mislead men as he has now. It was then enough to give, as Paul did, the simple and direct answer, telling men only what they must at once do. But this seems to be not enough now. So many delusions and perversions have bewildered and darkened the minds of men that they need often a great deal of instruction to lead them back to those simple views of the subject which prevailed at first. Hence the importance of showing what sinners must *not* do, if they intend to be saved.

1. *They must not imagine that they have nothing to do.* In Paul's time nobody seems to have thought of this. Then the doctrine of Universalism was not much developed. Men had not begun to dream that they should be saved without doing anything. They had not learned that sinners have nothing to do to be saved. If this idea, so current of late, had been rife at Phillippi, the question of our text would not have been asked. No trembling sinner would have cried out, *What must I do to be saved?*

If men imagine they have nothing to do, they are never likely to be saved. It is not in the nature of falsehood and lies to save men's souls, and surely nothing is more false than this notion. *Men know they have something to do to be saved.* Why, then, do they pretend that all men will be saved whether they do their duty, or constantly refuse to do it? The very idea is preposterous, and is entertained only by the most palpable outrage upon common sense and an enlightened conscience.

2. *You should not mistake what you have to do.* The duty required of sinners is very simple, and would be easily understood were it not for the false ideas that prevail as to what religion is, and as to the exact things which God requires as conditions of salvation. On these points erroneous opinions

prevail to a most alarming extent.   Hence the danger of mistake.   Beware lest you be deceived in a matter of so vital moment.

3. *Do not say or imagine that you cannot do what God requires.*   On the contrary, always assume that you can.   If you assume that you cannot, this very assumption will be fatal to your salvation.

4. *Do not procrastinate.*   As you ever intend or hope to be saved, you must set your face like a flint against this most pernicious delusion.   Probably no other mode of evading present duty has ever prevailed so extensively as this, or has destroyed so many souls.   Almost all men in Gospel lands intend to prepare for death—intend to repent and become religious before they die.   Even Universalists expect to become religious at some time—perhaps after death—perhaps after being purified from their sins by purgatorial fires ; but *somehow* they expect to become holy, for they know they *must* before they can see God and enjoy His presence.   But you will observe, they put this matter of becoming holy off to the most distant time possible.   Feeling a strong dislike to it now, they flatter themselves that God will take care that it shall be done up duly in the next world, how much soever they may frustrate His efforts to do it in this.   So long as it remains in their power to choose whether to become holy or not, they improve the time to enjoy sin ; and leave it with God to make them holy in the next world—if they can't prevent it there !   *Consistency* is *a jewel !*

And all those who put off being religious now in the cherished delusion of becoming so in some future time, whether in this world or the next, are acting out this same inconsistency.   You fondly hope *that* will occur which you are now doing your utmost to prevent.

So sinners by myriads press their way down to hell under this delusion.   They often, when pressed with the claims of

God, will even name the time when they will repent. It may be very near—perhaps as soon as they get home from the meeting, or as soon as the sermon is over ; or it may be more remote, as, for example, when they have finished their education, or become settled in life, or have made a little more property, or get ready to abandon some business of questionable morality ; but no matter whether the time set be near or remote, the delusion is fatal—the thought of procrastination is murder to the soul. Ah, such sinners are little aware that Satan himself has poured out his spirit upon them and is leading them whithersoever he will. He little cares whether they put off for a longer time or a shorter. If he can persuade them to a long delay, he likes it well ; if only to a short one, he feels quite sure he can renew the delay and get another extension—so it answers his purpose fully in the end.

Now mark, sinner, if you ever mean to be saved you must resist and grieve away this spirit of Satan. You must cease to procrastinate. You can never be converted so long as you operate only in the way of delaying and promising yourself that you will become religious at some future time. Did you ever bring anything to pass in your temporal business by procrastination ? Did procrastination ever begin, prosecute, and accomplish any important business ?

Suppose you have some business of vast consequence, involving your character, or your whole estate, or your life, to be transacted in Cleveland, but you do not know precisely how soon it *must* be done. It may be done with safety now, and with greater facility now than ever hereafter ; but it might possibly be done although you should delay a little time, but every moment's delay involves an absolute uncertainty of your being able to do it at all. You do not know but a single hour's delay will make you too late. Now in these circumstances what would a man of sense and discretion do ? Would he not be awake and up in an instant ?

Would he sleep on a matter of such moment, involving such risks and uncertainties? No. You know that the risk of a hundred dollars, pending on such conditions, would stir the warm blood of any man of business, and you could not tempt him to delay an hour. O, he would say, this is the great business to which I must attend, and everything else must give way. But suppose he should act as a sinner does about repentance, and promise himself that to-morrow will be as this day and much more abundant—and do nothing to-day, nor to-morrow, nor the next month, nor the next year—would you not think him beside himself? Would you expect his business to be done, his money to be secured, his interests to be promoted?

So the sinner accomplishes nothing but his own ruin so long as he procrastinates. Until he says—" Now is my time—*to-day* I will do all my duty "—he is only playing the fool and laying up his wages accordingly. O, it is infinite madness to defer a matter of such vast interest and of such perilous uncertainty!

5. If you would be saved *you must not wait for God to do what He commands you to do.*

God will surely do all that He can for your salvation. All that the nature of the case allows of His doing, He either has done or stands ready to do as soon as your position and course will allow Him to do it. Long before you were born He anticipated your wants as a sinner, and began on the most liberal scale to make provision for them. He gave His Son to die for you, thus doing all that need be done by way of an atonement. Of a long time past He has been shaping His providence so as to give you the requisite knowledge of duty —has sent you His Word and Spirit. Indeed, He has given you the highest possible evidence that He will be energetic and prompt on His part—as one in earnest for your salvation. You *know this*. What sinner in this house fears lest God should be negligent on His part in the matter of his salva-

tion ? Not one. No, many of you are not a little annoyed
that God should press you so earnestly and be so energetic in
the work of securing your salvation. And now can you
quiet your conscience with the excuse of waiting for God to do
your duty ?

The fact is, there are things for you to do which God can
not do for you. Those things which He has enjoined and
revealed as the conditions of your salvation, He cannot and
will not do Himself. If He could have done them Himself,
He would not have asked you to do them. Every sinner
ought to consider this. God requires of you repentance and
faith because it is naturally impossible that any one else but
you should do them. They are your own personal matters—
the voluntary exercises of your own mind ; and no other being
in heaven, earth, or hell, can do these things for you in your
stead. As far as substitution was naturally possible, God has
introduced it, as in the case of the atonement. He has never
hesitated to march up to meet and to bear all the self-denials
which the work of salvation has involved.

6. If you mean to be saved, *you must not wait for God to
do anything whatever.* There is nothing to be waited for.
God has either done all on His part already, or if anything
more remains, He is ready and waiting this moment for you
to do your duty that He may impart all needful grace.

7. *Do not flee to any refuge of lies.* Lies cannot save you.
It is truth, not lies, that alone can save. I have often
wondered how men could suppose that Universalism could
save any man.

Men must be sanctified by the truth. There is no plainer
teaching in the Bible than this, and no Bible doctrine is better
sustained by reason and the nature of the case.

Now does Universalism sanctify anybody ? Universalists
say you must be punished for your sins, and that thus they will
be put away—as if the fires of purgatory would thoroughly
consume all sin, and bring out the sinner pure. Is this

being sanctified *by the truth?* You might as well hope to be saved by eating liquid fire ! You might as well expect fire to purify your soul from sin in this world, as in the next ! Why not ?

It is amazing that men should hope to be sanctified and saved by this great error, or, indeed, by any error whatever. God says you must be sanctified *by the truth.* Suppose you could believe this delusion, would it make you holy? Do you believe that it would make you humble, heavenly-minded, sin-hating, benevolent ? Can you believe any such thing ? Be assured that Satan is only the father of lies, and he cannot save you—in fact, he would not if he could ; he intends his lies not to save you, but to destroy your very soul, and nothing could be more adapted to its purpose. Lies are only the natural poison of the soul. You take them at your peril !

8. *Don't seek for any self-indulgent method of salvation.*

The great effort among sinners has always been to be saved in some way of self-indulgence. They are slow to admit that self-denial is indispensable—that *total, unqualified self-denial is the condition of being saved.* I warn you against supposing that you can be saved in some easy, self-pleasing way. Men ought to know, and always assume, that it is naturally indispensable for selfishness to be utterly put away and its demands resisted and put down.

I often ask—Does the system of salvation which I preach so perfectly chime with the intuitions of my reason that I know from within myself that this Gospel is the thing I need ? Does it in all its parts and relations meet the demands of my intelligence ? Are its requisitions obviously just and right ? Does its prescribed conditions of salvation obviously befit man's moral position before God, and his moral relations to the government of God ?

To these and similar questions I am constrained to answer in the affirmative. The longer I live the more fully I see that the Gospel system is the only one that can alike meet the demands of the human intelligence, and supply the wants of man's sinning, depraved heart. The duties enjoined upon the sinner are just those things which I know must in the nature of the case be the conditions of salvation. Why, then, should any sinner think of being saved on any other con ditions? Why desire it even if it were ever so practicable?

9. *Don't imagine you will ever have a more favourable time.*

Impenitent sinners are prone to imagine that just now is by no means so convenient a season as may be expected hereafter. So they put off in hope of a better time. They think perhaps that they shall have more conviction, and fewer obstacles, and less hindrances. So thought Felix. He did not intend to forego salvation, any more than you do; but he was very busy just then—had certain ends to be secured which seemed peculiarly pressing, and so he begged to be excused on the promise of very faithful attention to the subject at the expected convenient season. But did the convenient season ever come? Never. Nor does it ever come to those who in like manner resist God's solemn call, and grieve away His Spirit. Thousands are now waiting in the pains of hell who said just as he did—" Go thy way for this time, when I have a convenient season I will call for thee." Oh, sinner, *when will your convenient season come?* Are you aware that no season will ever be *" convenient "* for you, unless God calls up your attention earnestly and solemnly to the subject? And can you expect Him to do this at the time of *your* choice, when you scorn His call at the time of *His* choice? Have you not heard Him say—"Because I have called, and ye refused, I have stretched out my hand, and no man regarded, but ye have set at nought all my counsel, and would none of my reproof; I also will laugh at your calamity; I will mock when your fear cometh. When your fear cometh as desolation, and your destruction cometh as a whirlwind, when distress and anguish cometh upon you; then shall they call upon me, but I will not answer; they shall seek me early, but they shall not find me." O, sinner, that will be a fearful and a final doom! And the myriad voices of God's universe will say, *amen*.

10. *Do not suppose that you will find another time as good, and one in which you can just as well repent as now.*

Many are ready to suppose that though there may be no better time for themselves, there will at least be one *as good*. Vain delusion! Sinner, you already owe ten thousand talents, and will you find it just as easy to be forgiven this debt while you are showing that you don't care how much and how long you augment it? In a case like this, where everything turns upon your securing the good-will of your creditor, do you hope to gain it by positively insulting him to his face?

Or take another view of the case. Your heart you know must one day relent for sin, or you are forever damned. You know also that each successive sin increases the hardness of your heart, and makes it a more difficult matter to repent. How, then, can you reasonably hope that a future time will be equally favourable for your repentance? When you have hardened your neck like an iron sinew, and made your heart like an adamant stone, can you hope that repentance will yet be as easy to you as ever?

You know, sinner, that God requires you to break off from your sins *now*. But you look up into His face and say to Him—"Lord, it is just as well to stop abusing Thee at some future convenient time. Lord, if I can only be saved at last, I shall think it all my gain to go on insulting and abusing Thee as long as it will possibly answer. And since Thou art so very compassionate and long-suffering, I think I may venture on in sin and rebellion against Thee yet these many months and years longer. Lord, don't hurry me—do let me have my way; let me abuse Thee if Thou pleasest, and spit in Thy face—all will be just as well if I only repent in season so as finally to be saved. I know, indeed, that Thou art entreating me to repent now, but I much prefer to wait a season, and it will be just as well to repent at some future time."

And now do you suppose that God will set His seal to this—that He will say—" You are right, sinner, I set my seal of approbation upon your course—it is well that you take so just views of your duty to your Maker and your Eather ; go on ; your course will ensure your salvation." Do you expect such a response from God as this ?

11. *If you ever expect to be saved, don't wait to see what others will do or say.*

I was lately astonished to find that a young lady here under conviction was in great trouble about what a beloved brother would think of her if she should give her heart to God. She knew her duty ; but he was impenitent, and how could she know what he would think if she should repent now ! It amounts to this. She would come before God and say—" O Thou great God, I know I ought to repent, but I can't ; for I don't know as my brother will like it. I know that he too is a sinner, and must repent or lose his soul, but I am much more afraid of his frown than I am of Thine, and I care more for his approbation than I do for Thine, and consequently, I dare not repent till he does ! " How shocking is this ! Strange that on such a subject men will ever ask— " What will others say of me ? " Are you amenable to God ? What, then, have others to say about your duty to Him ? God requires you and them also to repent, *and why don't you do it at once ?*

Not long since, as I was preaching abroad, one of the principal men of the city came to the meeting for inquiry, apparently much convicted and in great distress for his soul. But being a man of high political standing, and supposing himself to be very dependent upon his friends, he insisted that he must consult them, and have a regard for their feelings in this matter. I could not possibly beat him off from this ground, although I spent three hours in the effort. He seemed almost ready to repent—I thought he certianly would ; but he slipped away, relapsed by a perpetual backsliding, and I expect will be found at last among the lost in perdition. Would you not expect such a result if he tore himself away under such an excuse as that ?

O, sinner, you must not care what others say of you—let them say what they please. Remember, the question is between your own soul and God, and "He that is wise shall be wise for himself, and he that scorneth, he alone shall bear it." You must die for yourself, and for yourself must appear before God in judgment ! Go, young woman, ask your brother —" Can you answer for me when I come to the judgment? Can you pledge yourself that you can stand in my stead and answer for me there ?" Now until you have reason to believe that he can, it is wise for you to disregard his opinions if they stand at all in your way. Whoever interposes any objection to your immediate repentance, fail not to ask him— Can you shield my soul in the judgment ? If I can be assured that you can and will, I will make you my Saviour ; but if not, then I must attend to my own salvation, and leave you to attend to yours.

I never shall forget the scene which occured while my own mind was turning upon this great point. Seeking a retired place for prayer, I went into a deep grove, found a perfectly secluded spot behind some large logs, and knelt down. All suddenly, a leaf rustled and I sprang, for somebody must be coming and I shall be seen here at prayer. I had not been aware that I cared what others said of me, but looking back upon my exercises of mind here, I could see that I did care infinitely too much what others thought of me.

Closing my eyes again for prayer, I heard a rustling leaf again, and then the thought came over me like a wave of the sea—" I *am* ashamed of confessing my sin !" What ! thought I, ashamed of being found speaking with God ! O, how ashamed I felt of this shame ! I can never describe the strong and overpowering impression which this thought made on my mind. I cried aloud at the very top of my voice, for I felt that though all the men on earth and all the devils in hell were present to hear and see me I would not shrink and would not cease to cry unto God ; for what is it to me if others see me seeking the face of my God and Saviour ? I am hastening to the judgment :—*there* I shall not be ashamed to have the Judge my friend. *There* I shall not be ashamed to have sought His face and His pardon here. *There* will be no shrinking away from the gaze of the universe. O, if sinners at the judgment could shrink away, how gladly would they ; but they cannot ! Nor can they stand there in each other's places to answer for each other's sins. That young woman, can she say then—O, my brother, you must answer for me ; for to please you, I rejected Christ and lost my soul ? That brother is himself a guilty rebel, confounded, and agonized, and quailing before the awful Judge, and how can he befriend you in such an awful hour ! Fear not his displeasure now, but rather warn him while you can, to escape for his life ere the wrath of the Lord wax hot against him, and there be no remedy.

12. If you would be saved, *you must not indulge prejudices against either God, or His ministers, or against Christians, or against anything religious.*

There are some persons of peculiar temperament who are greatly in danger of losing their souls because they are tempted to strong prejudices. Once committed either in favour of or against any persons or things they are exceedingly apt to become so fixed as never more to be really honest. And when these persons or things in regard to which they become committed, are so connected with religion, that their prejudices stand arrayed against their fulfilling the great conditions of salvation, the effect can be nothing else than ruinous. For it is naturally indispensable to salvation that you should be entirely honest.   Your soul must act before God in the open sincerity of truth, or you cannot be converted.

I have known persons in revivals to remain a long time under great conviction, without submitting themselves to God, and by careful inquiry I have found them wholly hedged in by their prejudices, and yet so blind to this fact that they would not admit that they had any prejudice at all.   In my observation of convicted sinners, I have found this among the most common obstacles in the way of the salvation of souls.   Men become committed against religion, and remaining in this state it is naturally impossible that they should repent.   God will not humour your prejudices, or lower His prescribed conditions of salvation to accommodate your feelings.

Again, you must give up all hostile feelings in cases where you have been really injured.   Sometimes I have seen persons evidently shut out from the kingdom of heaven, because having been really injured, they would not forgive and forget, but maintained such a spirit of resistance and revenge, that they could not, in the nature of the case, repent of the sin toward God, nor could God forgive them.   Of course they lost heaven.   I have heard men say—" I cannot forgive—I will not forgive—I have been injured, and I never will forgive that wrong."   Now mark : you must not hold on to such feelings ; if you do, you cannot be saved.

Again, you must not suffer yourself to be stumbled by the prejudices of others.   I have often been struck with the state of things in families, where the parents or older persons had prejudices against the minister, and have wondered why those parents were not more wise than to lay stumbling-blocks before their children to ruin their souls.   This is often the true reason why children are not converted.   Their minds are turned against the Gospel, by being turned against those from whom they hear it preached.   I would rather have persons come into my family, and curse and swear before my children, than to have them speak against those who preach to them the Gospel. Therefore I say to all parents—take care what you say, if you would not shut the gate of heaven against your children !

Again, do not allow yourself to take some fixed position, and then suffer the stand you have taken to debar you from doing any obvious duty. Persons sometimes allow themselves to be committed against taking what is called " the anxious seat ;" and consequently they refuse to go forward under circumstances when it is obviously proper that they should, and where their refusal to do so, places them in an attitude unfavourable, and perhaps fatal to their conversion. Let every sinner beware of this !

Again, do not hold on to anything about which you have any doubt of its lawfulness or propriety. Cases often occur in which persons are not fully satisfied that a thing is wrong, and yet are not satisfied that it is right. Now in cases of this sort it should not be enough to say—" such and such Christians do so ;" you ought to have better reasons than this for your course of conduct. If you ever expect to be saved, you must abandon all practices which you even suspect to be wrong. This principle seems to be involved in the passage, " He that doubteth is damned if he eat ; for whatsoever is not of faith is sin." To do that which is of doubtful propriety is to allow yourself to tamper with the divine authority, and cannot fail to break down in your mind that solemn dread of sinning which, if you would ever be saved, you must carefully cherish.

Again, if you would be saved, do not look at professors and wait for them to become engaged as they should be in the great work of God. If they are not what they ought to be, let them alone. Let them bear their own awful responsibility. It often happens that convicted sinners compare themselves with professed Christians, and excuse themselves for delaying their duty, because professed Christians are delaying theirs. Sinners must not do this if they would ever be saved. It is very probable that you will always find guilty professors enough to stumble over into hell if you will allow yourself to do so.

But on the other hand, many professors may not be nearly so bad as you suppose, and you must not be censorious, putting the worst constructions upon their conduct. You have other work to do than this. Let them stand or fall to their own master. Unless you abandon the practice of picking flaws in the conduct of professed Christians, it is utterly impossible that you should be saved.

Again, do not depend upon professors—on their prayers or influence in any way. I have known children hang a long time upon the prayers of their parents, putting those prayers in the place of Jesus Christ, or at least in the place of their own present efforts to do their duty. Now this course pleases Satan entirely. He would ask nothing more to make sure of you. Therefore, depend on no prayers—not even those of the holiest Christians on earth. The matter of your conversion lies between yourself and God alone, as really as if you were the only sinner in all the world, or as if there were no other beings in the universe but yourself and your God.

Do not *seek for any apology or excuse whatever*. I dwell upon this and urge it the more because I so often find persons resting on some excuse without being themselves aware of it. In conversation with them upon their spiritual state, I see this and say, " There you are resting on that excuse." " Am I ?" say they, " I did not know it."

Do not seek for stumbling-blocks. Sinners, a little disturbed in their stupidity, begin to cast about for stumbling-blocks for self-vindication. All at once they become wide awake to the faults of professors, as if they had to bear the care of all the churches. The real fact is, they are all engaged to find something to which they can take exception, so that they can thereby blunt the keen edge of truth upon their own consciences. This never helps along their own salvation.

Do not tempt the forbearance of God. If you do, you are in the utmost danger of being given over forever. Do not presume that you may go on yet longer in your sins, and still find the gate of mercy. This presumption has paved the way for the ruin of many souls.

Do not despair of salvation and settle down in unbelief, saying, "There is no mercy for me." You must not despair in any such sense as to shut yourself out from the kingdom. You may well despair of being saved without Christ and without repentance; but you are bound to believe the Gospel; and to do this is to believe the glad tidings that Jesus Christ has come to save sinners, even the chief, and that "Him that cometh to Him He will in no wise cast out." You have no right to disbelieve this, and act as if there were no truth in it.

You must not wait for more conviction. Why do you need any more? You know your guilt and know your present duty. Nothing can be more preposterous, therefore, than to wait for more conviction. If you did not know that you are a sinner, or that you are guilty for sin, there might be some fitness in seeking for conviction of the truth on these points.

Do not wait for more or for different feelings. Sinners are often saying—"I must feel differently before I can come to Christ," or—"I must have *more* feeling." As if this were the great thing which God requires of them. In this they are altogether mistaken.

Do not wait to be better prepared. While you wait you are growing worse and worse, and are fast rendering your salvation impossible.

Don't wait for God to change your heart. Why should

you wait for Him to do what He has commanded you to do, and waits for you to do in obedience to His command ?

Don't try to recommend yourself to God by prayers or tears or by anything else whatsoever. Do you suppose your prayers lay God under any obligation to forgive you ? Suppose you owed a man five hundred talents, and should go a hundred times a week and beg him to remit to you this debt ; and then should enter your prayers in account against your creditor, as so much claim against him. Suppose you should pursue this course till you had cancelled the debt, as you suppose— could you hope to prove anything by this course except that you were mad ? And yet sinners seem to suppose that their many prayers and tears lay the Lord under real obligation to them to forgive them.

Never rely on anything else whatever than Jesus Christ, and Him crucified. It is preposterous for you to hope, as many do, to make some propitiation by your own sufferings. In my early experience I thought I could not expect to be converted at once, but must be bowed down a long time. I said to myself—" God will not pity me till I feel worse than I do now. I can't expect Him to forgive me till I feel a greater agony of soul than this." Not even if I could have gone on augmenting my sufferings till they equalled the miseries of hell, it could not have changed God. The fact is, God does not ask of you that you should suffer. Your sufferings cannot in the nature of the case avail for atonement. Why, therefore, should you attempt to thrust aside the system of God's providing, and thrust in one of your own ?

There is another view of the case. The thing God demands of you is that you should bow your stubborn will to Him. Just as a child in the attitude of disobedience, and required to submit, might fall to weeping and groaning, and to every expression of agony, and might even torture himself, in hope of moving the pity of his father, but all the time refuses to submit to parental authority. He would be very glad to put his own sufferings in the place of the submission demanded. This is what the sinner is doing. He would fain put his own sufferings in the place of submission to God, and move the pity of the Lord so much that He would recede from the hard condition of repentance and submission.

If you would be saved you must not listen at all to those who pity you, and who impliedly take your part against God, and try to make you think you are not so bad as you are. I once knew a woman who, after a long season of distressing conviction, fell into great despair ; her health sank, and she seemed about to die. All this time she found no relief, but seemed only to wax worse and worse, sinking down in stern and awful despair. Her friends, instead of dealing plainly and faithfully with her, and probing her guilty heart to the bottom, had taken the course of pitying her, and almost complained of the Lord that He would not have compassion on the poor agonized, dying woman. At length, as she seemed in the last stages of life—so weak as to be scarcely able to speak in a low voice, there happened in a minister who better understood how to deal with convicted sinners. The woman's friends cautioned him to deal very carefully with her, as she was in a dreadful state and greatly to be pitied ; but he judged it best to deal with her very faithfully. As he approached her bed-side, she raised her faint voice and begged for a little water. "Unless you repent, you will soon be," said he, "where there is not a drop of water to cool your tongue." "O," she cried, "*must I go down to hell?*" "Yes, you must, and you will, soon, unless you repent and submit to God. Why don't you repent and submit immediately ?" "O," she replied, "it is an awful thing to go to hell !" "Yes, and for that very reason Christ has provided an atonement through Jesus Christ, but *you won't accept it*. He brings the cup of salvation to your lips, and you thrust it away. Why will you

do this ? Why will you persist in being an enemy of God
and scorn His offered salvation, when you might become His
friend and have salvation if you would ? "

This was the strain of their conversation, and its result was,
that the woman saw her guilt and her duty, and turning to
the Lord, found pardon and peace.

Therefore I say, if your conscience convicts you of sin,
don't let anybody take your part against God. Your wound
needs not a plaster, but a *probe*. Don't fear the probe ; it is
the only thing that can save you. Don't seek to hide your
guilt, or veil your eyes from seeing it, nor be afraid to know
the worst, for you must know the very worst, and the sooner
you know it the better. I warn you, don't look after some
physician to give you an opiate, for you don't need it. Shun,
as you would. death itself, all those who would speak to you
smooth things and prophesy deceits. They would surely ruin
your soul.

Again, do not suppose that if you become a Christian, it will
interfere with any of the necessary or appropriate duties of
life, or with anything whatever to which you ought to attend.
No ; religion never interferes with any real duty. So far is
this from being the case, that in fact a proper attention to
your various duties is indispensable to your being religious.
You cannot serve God without.

Moreover, if you would be saved you must not give heed to
anything that would hinder you. It is infinitely important
that your soul should be saved. No consideration thrown in
your way should be allowed to have the weight of a straw or
a feather. Jesus Christ has illustrated and enforced this by
several parables, especially in the one which compares the
kingdom of heaven to " a merchant-man seeking goodly pearls,
who when he had found one pearl of great price went and sold
all that he had and bought it." In another parable, the kingdom of heaven is said to be " like treasure hid in a field,
which, when a man hath found, he hideth, and for joy thereof

goeth and selleth all that he hath and buyeth that field." Thus forcibly are men taught that they must be ready to make any sacrifice whatever which may be requisite in order to gain the kingdom of heaven.

Again, you *must not seek religion selfishly.* You must not make your own salvation or happiness the supreme end. Beware, for if you make this your supreme end you will get a false hope, and will probably glide along down the pathway of the hypocrite into the deepest hell.

II. *What sinners must do to be saved.*

1. You *must understand what you have to do.* It is of the utmost importance that you should see this clearly. You need to know that you must return to God, and to understand what this means. The difficulty between yourself and God is that you have stolen yourself and run away from His service. You belong of right to God. He created you for Himself, and hence had a perfectly righteous claim to the homage of your heart, and the service of your life. But you, instead of living to meet His claims, have run away—have deserted from God's service, and have lived to please yourself. Now your duty is to return and restore yourself to God.

2. *You must return and confess your sins to God.* You must confess that you have been all wrong, and that God has been all right. Go before the Lord and lay open the depth of your guilt. Tell Him you deserve just as much damnation as He has threatened.

These confessions are naturally indispensable to your being forgiven. In accordance with this the Lord says, "If then their uncircumcised hearts be humbled, and they then *accept of the punishment* of their iniquity, then will I remember my covenant." Then God can forgive. But so long as you controvert this point, and will not concede that God is right, or admit that you are wrong, He can never forgive you.

You must moreover confess to man if you have injured

any one. And is it not a fact that you have injured some, and perhaps many of your fellow-men? Have you not slandered your neighbour and said things which you have no right to say? Have you not in some instances, which you could call to mind if you would, lied to them, or about them, or covered up or perverted the truth; and have you not been willing that others should have false impressions of you or of your conduct? If so, you must renounce all such iniquity, for "He that covereth his sins shall not prosper; while he that confesseth and forsaketh them shall find mercy." And, furthermore, you must not only confess your sins to God and to the men you have injured, but you must also *make restitution.* You have not taken the position of a penitent before God and man until you have done this also. God cannot treat you as a penitent until you have done it. I do not mean by this that God cannot forgive you until you have carried into effect your purpose of restitution by finishing the outward act, for sometimes it may demand time, and may in some cases be itself impossible to you. But the purpose must be sincere and thorough before you can be forgiven of God.

3. You *must renounce yourself.* In this is implied,—

(1.) That you renounce your own righteousness, forever discarding the very idea of having any righteousness in yourself.

(2.) That you forever relinquish the idea of *having done any good* which ought to commend you to God, or be ever thought of as a ground of your justification.

(3.) That you *renounce your own will,* and be ever ready to say not in word only, but in heart—" Thy will be done, on earth as it is in heaven." You must consent most heartily that God's will shall be your supreme law.

(4.) That you renounce *your own way* and let God have His own way in everything. Never suffer yourself to fret and be rasped by anything whatever; for since God's agency extends to all events, you ought to recognize His hand in all things ; and of course to fret at anything whatever is to fret againt God who has at least *permitted* that thing to occur as it does. So long, therefore, as you suffer yourself to fret, you are not right with God. You must become before God as a little child, subdued and trustful at His feet. Let the weather be fair or foul, consent that God should have His way. Let all things go well with you, or as men call it, *ill ;* yet let God do His pleasure, and let it be your part to submit in perfect resignation. Until you take this ground you cannot be saved.

4. You *must come to Christ.* You must accept of Christ really and fully *as your Saviour.* Renouncing all thought of depending on anything you have done or can do, you must accept of Christ as your atoning sacrifice, and as your ever-living Mediator before God. Without the least qualification or reserve you must place yourself under His wing as your Saviour.

5. You *must seek supremely to please Christ, and not yourself.* It is naturally impossible that you should be saved until you come into this attitude of mind—until you are so well pleased with Christ in all respects as to find your pleasure in doing His. It is in the nature of things impossible that you should be happy in any other state of mind, or unhappy in this. For, His pleasure is infinitely good and right. When, therefore, His good pleasure becomes your good pleasure, and your will harmonizes entirely with His, then you will be happy for the same reason that He is happy, and you cannot fail of being happy any more than Jesus Christ can. And this becoming supremely happy in God's will is essentially the idea of salvation. In this state of mind *you are saved.* Out of it you cannot be.

It has often struck my mind with great force, that many professors of religion are deplorably and utterly mistaken on this point. Their real feeling is that Christ's service is an iron collar—an insufferably hard yoke.   Hence, they labour exceedingly to throw off some of this burden.   They try to make it out that Christ does not require much, if any, self-denial—much, if any, deviation from the course of worldliness and sin.   O, if they could only get the standard of Christian duty quite down to a level with the fashions and customs of this world!   How much easier then to live a Christian life and wear Christ's yoke!

But taking Christ's yoke as it really is, it becomes in their view an iron collar.   Doing the will of Christ, instead of their own, is a hard business.   Now if doing Christ's will *is* religion, (and who can doubt it?) then they only need enough of it; and *in their state of mind* they will be supremely wretched.   Let me ask those who groan under the idea that they *must* be religious—who deem it awful hard—but they *must*—how much religion of this kind would it take to make hell?   Surely not much!   When it gives you no joy to do God's pleasure, and yet you are shut up to the doing of His pleasure is the only way to be saved, and are thereby perpetually dragooned into the doing of what you hate, as the only means of escaping hell, would not this be itself a hell?   Can you not see that in this state of mind you are not saved and cannot be?

To be saved you must come into a state of mind in which you will ask no higher joy than to do God's pleasure. This alone will be forever enough to fill your cup to over-flowing.

You *must have all confidence in Christ, or you cannot be saved*.   You must absolutely believe in Him—believe all His words of promise.   They were given you to be believed, and unless you believe them they can do you no good at all. So far from helping you without you exercise faith in them, they will only aggravate your guilt for unbelief.   God would be believed when He speaks in love to lost sinners.   He gave them these "exceeding great and precious promises, that they, by faith in them, might escape the corruption that is in the world through lust." But thousands of professors of religion know not how to use these promises, and as to them or any profitable use *they make*, the promises might as well have been written on the sands of the sea.

Sinners, too, will go down to hell in unbroken masses, unless they believe and take hold of God by faith in His promise. O, His awful wrath is out against them! And He says—" I would go through them, I would burn them up together ; *or let him take hold of My strength*, that he may make peace with Me; and he shall make peace with Me." Yes, let him stir up himself and take hold of My arm, strong to save, and then he may make peace with Me. Do you ask how take hold? By faith. Yes, *by faith ;* believe His words and *take hold ;* take hold of His strong arm and swing right out over hell, and don't be afraid any more than if there were no hell.

But you say—I do believe, and yet I am not saved. No, you don't believe. A woman said to me—" I believe, I know I do, and yet here I am in my sins." No, said I, you don't. Have you as much confidence in God as you would have in me if I had promised you a dollar? Do you ever pray to God? And, if so, do you come with any such confidence as you would have if you came to me to ask for a promised dollar? Oh, until you have as much faith in God as this, aye and more—until you have more confidence in God than you would have in ten thousand men, your faith does not honour God, and you cannot hope to please Him. You must say — " Let God be true though every man be a liar."

But you say—" O, I am a sinner, and how can I believe?" I know you are a sinner, and so are all men to whom God has given these promises. " O, but I am a *great sinner !*" Well, " It is a faithful saying and worthy of all acceptation, that Jesus Christ came into the world to save sinners, of whom," Paul says, "I am the chief." So you need not despair.

7. You must *forsake all that you have,* or you cannot be Christ's disciple. There must be absolute and total *self-denial.*

By this I do not mean that you are never to eat again, or never again to clothe yourself, or never more enjoy the society of your friends—no, not this; but that you should cease entirely from using any of these enjoyments selfishly. You must no longer think to own yourself—your time, your possessions, or anything you have ever called your own. All these things you must hold as God's, not yours. In this sense you are to forsake all that you have, namely, in the sense of laying all upon God's altar to be devoted supremely and only to His service. When you come back to God for pardon and salvation, come with all you have to lay all at his feet. Come with your body, to offer it as a living sacrifice upon His altar. Come with your soul and all its powers, and yield them in willing consecration to your God and Saviour. Come, bring them all along—everything, body, soul, intellect, imagination, acquirements—all, without reserve. Do you say—Must I bring them *all?* Yes, all—absolutely ALL; do not keep back anything—don't sin against your own soul, like Ananias and Sapphira, by keeping back a part, but renounce your own claim to everything, and recognize God's right to all. Say— Lord, these things are not mine. I had stolen them, but they were never mine. They were always Thine; I'll have them no longer. Lord, these things are all Thine, henceforth and forever. Now, what wilt Thou have me to do? I have no business of my own to do—I am wholly at Thy disposal. Lord, what work hast Thou for me to do?

In this spirit you must renounce the world, the flesh, and Satan. Your fellowship is henceforth to be with Christ, and not with those objects. You are to live for Christ, and not for the world, the flesh, or the devil.

8. You *must believe the record God hath given of His Son.*
He that believes not does not receive the record—does not set
to his seal that God is true. " This is the record that God
has given us eternal life, and this life is in His Son." The
condition of your having it is that you believe the record, and
of course that you act accordingly. Suppose here is a poor
man living at your next door, and the mail brings him a letter
stating that a rich man has died in England, leaving him
100,000 pounds sterling, and the cashier of a neighbouring
bank writes him that he has received the amount on deposit
for him, and holds it subject to his order. Well, the poor
man says, I can't believe the record. I can't believe there
ever was any such rich man; I can't believe there is 100,000
pounds for me. So he must live and die as poor as Lazarus,
because he won't believe the record.

Now, mark; this is just the case with the unbelieving
sinner. God has given you eternal life, and it waits your
order; but you don't get it because you will not believe, and
therefore will not make out the order, and present in due form
the application.

Ah, but you say, I must have some feeling before I can
believe—how can I believe till I have the feeling? So the
poor man might say—How can I believe that the 100,000
pounds is mine; I have not got a farthing of it now ;
I am as poor as ever. Yes, you are poor because you
will not believe. If you would believe, you might go and buy
out every store in this country. Still you cry, I am as poor
as ever. I can't believe it; see my poor worn clothes—I
was never more ragged in my life; I have not a particle of
the feeling and the comforts of a rich man. So the sinner
can't believe till he gets the inward experience ! He must
wait to have some of the feeling of a saved sinner before he
can believe the record and take hold of the salvation ! Preposterous enough! So the poor man must wait to get his
new clothes and fine house before he can believe his documents

and draw for his money. Of course he dooms himself to everlasting poverty, although mountains of gold were all his own.

Now, sinner, you must understand this. Why should you be lost when eternal life is bought and offered you by the last will and testament of the Lord Jesus Christ? Will you not believe the record and draw for the amount at once! Do for mercy's sake understand this and not lose heaven by your own folly!

I must conclude by saying, that if you would be saved you must accept a *prepared salvation,* one already prepared and full, and present. You must be willing to give up all your sins, and be saved from them, *all, now and henceforth!* Until you consent to this, you cannot be saved at all. Many would be willing to be saved in heaven, if they might hold on to some sins while on earth—or rather they *think* they would like heaven on such terms. But the fact is, they would as much dislike a pure heart and a holy life in heaven as they do on earth, and they deceive themselves utterly in supposing that they are ready or even willing to go to such a heaven as God has prepared for His people. No, there can be no heaven except for those who accept a salvation *from all sin* in this world. They must take the Gospel as a system which holds no compromise with sin—which contemplates full deliverance from sin even now, and makes provision accordingly. Any other gospel is not the true one, and to accept of Christ's Gospel in any other sense is not to accept it all. Its first and its last condition is *sworn and eternal renunciation of all sin.*